The Vowed Life

Other books from the Littlemore Group

Praying for England: Priestly Presence in Contemporary Culture, edited by Samuel Wells and Sarah Coakley.

Fear and Friendship: Anglicans Engaging with Islam, edited by Frances Ward and Sarah Coakley.

For God's Sake: Re-Imagining Priesthood and Prayer in a Changing Church, edited by Jessica Martin and Sarah Coakley.

Holy Attention: Preaching in Today's Church, edited by Frances Ward and Richard Sudworth.

The Vowed Life

The Promise and Demand of Baptism

Edited by

Sarah Coakley

and

Matthew Bullimore

CANTERBURY
PRESS
Norwich

First published in 2023 by the Canterbury Press Norwich
Editorial office
3rd Floor, Invicta House
108–114 Golden Lane
London EC1Y 0TG, UK

www.canterburypress.co.uk

Canterbury Press is an imprint of Hymns Ancient & Modern Ltd
(a registered charity)

Acknowledgement is made for permission to use quotations
from T. S. Eliot, 1942, 'Little Gidding', in *Four Quartets*,
London: Faber and Faber.

British Library Cataloguing in Publication data

A catalogue record for this book is available
from the British Library

978-1-78622-189-6

Typeset by Regent Typesetting
Printed and bound in Great Britain by
CPI Group (UK) Ltd

Contents

Part II Contemporary Anglican Reflections on the 'Vowed Life' of Religious Community

List of Contributors

The Revd Dr Matthew Bullimore is Chaplain of Corpus Christi College, Cambridge, and was formerly Vicar of Royston, St John the Baptist, and Felkirk, St Peter.

The Revd Professor Sarah Coakley served as part-time curate in the parish of St Mary and St Nicholas, Littlemore, from 2000 to 2009, during which time (2005) the 'Littlemore Group' was founded. More recently she has been an honorary canon at Ely Cathedral, and (in the United States) an assisting priest and theologian-in-residence at the parish of the Ascension and St Agnes, Washington DC. In her academic life as a theologian and philosopher of religion she was formerly Mallinckrodt Professor of Divinity at Harvard Divinity School (1995–2007), and Norris-Hulse Professor of Divinity at the University of Cambridge (2007–18).

Dr Petà Dunstan is a Fellow of St Edmund's College, University of Cambridge, and was for 30 years the Librarian of the Faculty of Divinity at the University. She is a historian writing on Anglican Religious life and serves on the Advisory Council for Religious Communities. She has taught on the inter-novitiate course for communities in the UK since its inception in 2012, as well as being a trustee for and advisor to several communities. She is also the founder and editor of the Anglican Religious Life Year Book (now online) which links Anglican communities throughout the world.

The Revd Dr Ben Edson is Director of St Peter's House, the Chaplaincy to the Universities of Manchester and the Royal Northern College of Music.

The Ven. Dr Alex Hughes is Archdeacon of Cambridge, and was formerly Vicar of Southsea, St Luke and St Peter.

The Revd Dr Victoria Johnson is Canon Precentor, York Minster, and was formerly Residentiary Canon, Ely Cathedral; earlier she had been Priest-in-Charge of Flixton, St Michael.

Sr Judith, SLG is a member of the Community of the Sisters of the Love of God, Fairacres, Oxford.

The Revd Dr Joel Love is Vicar of Rochester, St Peter & St Margaret, and Priest Vicar, Rochester Cathedral.

The Revd Dr Rachel Mann is Area Dean of Bury & Rossendale, and was formerly Rector of Burnage, St Nicholas.

The Revd Dr Jessica Martin is Residentiary Canon, Ely Cathedral. She was previously Priest-in-Charge of Duxford, St Peter, of Hinxton, St Mary & St John, of Ickleton, St Mary Magdalene, of Whittlesford, St Mary and St Andrew, and of Pampisford, St John the Baptist.

The Revd Dr Edmund Newey is Rector of Rugby, St Andrew, and was formerly Sub-Dean of Oxford, Christ Church.

The Revd Dr Richard Sudworth is Secretary for Inter Religious Affairs to the Archbishop of Canterbury, and was formerly Priest-in-Charge of Sparkbrook, Christ Church.

The Revd Dr Frances Ward is Priest-in Charge of Workington, St John, and of Workington, St Michael, and was formerly Chair of the Little Gidding Trust, 2012–19. She is Dean Emerita of St Edmundsbury Cathedral.

The Most Revd Justin Welby is Archbishop of Canterbury.

Introduction: The Vowed Life – Its Demand and Promise

SARAH COAKLEY AND
MATTHEW BULLIMORE

> 'Simply having to live together with people you wouldn't have chosen yourself, and to pray together three times a day – this gives you a whole new sense of what Christian "community" is, and could be.'

> 'You know something is happening to you but you can't adequately describe it – it's a going deeper, a new discovery of what "Church" could be and mean for others.'

So spoke two of the young members of the St Anselm Community at Lambeth Palace, when we visited and interviewed them a while ago. As of this year (2023), that new experiment in monastic living is into its eighth annual cohort, and has somehow survived – though not without difficulty – the multiple challenges of the global pandemic. It brings young ecumenical Christians (aged 20–35) from across the world into a year's experimental life together, a life of prayer and service and community-building which leaves those who stay with it seemingly strangely changed in their perspective on the world and the Church. It was the brain-child of the current Archbishop of Canterbury, Justin Welby, for whom the conviction that a new Religious community at Lambeth was urgently needed was a missional *leitmotif* from the start of his arch-episcopate: 'There has never been a renewal of the Church without a renewal of prayer and the religious life', as he put it.[1] And so he made it happen at Lambeth itself.

But why this new and contemporary interest in a short-term (and frankly, somewhat artificially confected) monastic life for young people, precisely at the moment when the more stringent demands of the 'old' monasticism, with its demanding life-long vows of poverty, chastity and obedience, seem to offend and even repel some of our deepest cultural mores? As recent experiments in 'new monasticism' have serially taken flight, and an interest in spirituality, guided retreats, and tertiary commitments to Religious life has escalated, only a few of the classic Anglican Religious communities in the United Kingdom have re-burgeoned and attracted younger members, while others are visibly dying or have necessarily re-configured into new shapes of witness.

It is this core paradox about vowed commitment that this book seeks to reflect upon, first and foremost, and to illumine spiritually and theologically. But we also seek to look at the wider implications of this paradox for the Church more generally and for its other vows and promises. Why are the evident demands of monastic vows today simultaneously so strangely alluring to many, and yet also equally repellent or perplexing to others, in a culture of supposed ongoing secularization, seeming 'erotic' carelessness, and great existential fearfulness for the future? What is the *meaning* of any vow in a religious context, and how can it both bind and free the one who makes it?[2] More fundamentally, how do the vows made in the sacrament of baptism (the anchor for any further vows thereafter in a Christian's life) relate to, and unfold into, the vows and commitments of the sacrament of confirmation (if it is undergone at all, these days), and then – rather differently – into the specific,

1 Welby, Justin, 2013, 'ABC's First Priority: The Renewal of Prayer and the Religious Life', *New Wine Magazine*, 58, p. 42. Cited and anticipatorily discussed in Martin, Jessica and Coakley, Sarah (eds), *For God's Sake: Re-Imagining Priesthood and Prayer in a Changing Church*, Norwich: Canterbury Press, pp. 175–6. See also Petà Dunstan's reference to the same text in Chapter 1, below.

2 Sister Judith, SLG, directly confronts this question in Chapter 6, below.

and we might say vocationally *intensified*, vows of marriage, ordination, or the Religious life?

The Littlemore Group (a group of scholar-priests and Religious deeply committed to the parochial life of the Church of England) has been musing on these issues, perceived by us also to be central ones for the Church and its future, from almost the moment of our own inception in 2005.[3] What follow in this book are chapters on these topics which have evolved over the last several years, have been intensively debated between us, and have been particularly animated and inspired by our interaction with a wide range of old monastic Anglican Religious (including one in our number), as well as by some members of the new monastic movements from whom we have also learned so much as well.

It may then be worthwhile to underscore immediately what our central theological conclusions in this book are, after these years of reflection; for they have not emerged without struggle, prayer, genuine mutual differences, and deep concern for the Church's ongoing life and mission. Cumulatively, however, the chapters that follow mount a set of core arguments in response to the questions already raised, and the sharp edge of those arguments which emerge through the book will doubtless not escape controversy. At the very least they deserve a clear enunciation at the outset.

The Central Theses of this Book: The 'Vowed Life' and its Implications

First, our response to the paradox of the simultaneous cultural allure and cultural distaste towards monastic vows is itself two-sided, and thus forms a sort of crux that runs through this book as a whole.

3 Our founding meeting (as described in Wells, Samuel and Sarah Coakley (eds), 2008, *Praying for England: Priestly Presence in Contemporary Culture*, London: Continuum, pp. 187–90) took place in Littlemore, Oxford, partly in John Henry Newman's 'College' and also at the Anglican church he built there; the return to a parochial life of measured prayer and coordinated pastoral ministry was key to the formation and goals of our group.

On the one hand, we are inclined to the view that the Church of England in recent years, doubtless out of a sense of panic at its numerical decline and apparent cultural marginalization, has become so fearful of making *demands* on its dwindling parish membership, that a great longing has emerged – in what is surely an inevitable spiritual riposte – for forms of life that are transcendently and manifestly life-*changing*, demanding in the most profound sense in relation to human life and its goals. 'It is a fearful thing to fall into the hands of the living God', warns the author to the epistle to the Hebrews (Heb. 10.31); and yet so also, as Evelyn Underhill famously reminded Archbishop Lang in advance of the Lambeth Conference of 1930, it is this same God that people *want*, God being the 'interesting thing' that they seek when they turn away in dissatisfaction from secular life in search of something deeper.[4] New monasticisms characteristically offer precisely such a set of interesting demands in relation to this God, usually a whole way of life with regular practices, promises and requirements which shape the day afresh and bind adherents into new forms of community.

But a profound question already presses awkwardly underneath this observation here: should not simply becoming a *Christian* (in baptism, but especially in confirmation, if baptism was received passively as a child) itself present such a set of life-changing and transcendent demands? In other words, is the contemporary longing for monastic life perhaps a displaced desire for something that should itself be basic to Christian life from the outset?[5] Herein, perhaps, we may locate something of the contemporary longing, the allure, of Religious vows: for if it is *God* we want, we know that this is 'fearful' and will likely cost us 'nothing less than everything'.

But on the other hand, and secondly, we have had to ask ourselves whether the widespread current *distaste* towards life-vows in the old monasticisms is also a manifestation of something deeper than first appears. Is it perhaps at base a fear of loss of optionality and freedom in the modern sense (over against

4 See the brief discussion of Underhill's historic challenge in Wells et al., *Praying for England*, pp. 7–8.

5 Alex Hughes explores this line of thought in Chapter 3, below.

monastic obedience)? Or is it a suspicion about the vow of chastity (in the form of celibacy), especially, as merely a front for sexual evasion or something worse? Or is it a presumption that something as *binding* as these particular vows (particularly in their requirement of poverty and the relinquishment of wealth, status and belongings) might smother any long-term hope of comfort, satisfaction or personal fulfilment? Scepticism abounds on all these fronts, and it has to be faced. But the fact is that the distinctive, counter-cultural, spiritual *fruitfulness* of monasticism as a life-long undertaking has always had to be seen to be believed: as Gregory of Nyssa once put it, in the late-fourth century, there have to be living and alluring personal examples of it, such that we can 'catch the halo'.[6] Otherwise the cynicism, fear and suspicion of the detractors simply mount up against a way of life so obviously at odds with currently accepted human goals and presumptions.

This initial set of reflections may thus cause us to re-express our original paradox: There is a great *longing* for demanding and life-changing vows in Christian life; but there is equally a *fear* that they may be simply impossible or delusory, or that any failure in them will topple the credibility of the whole Christian enterprise.

So how can we think further about this paradox for today, both creatively and theologically, and especially within the Church of England?

One of the most fruitful approaches to this question we have found in the work for this book is in re-excavating the *relationship* of the discrete vows in the different forms of vowed life the Anglican tradition classically presents to us. Not much theological work has been done on this matter of late, we have found. But this quest has enabled us to get a rich, historical perspective on our key paradox. In the earliest prayer books and ordinals of the reformed English tradition (as we explore in several chapters later in this book), this work of coordination was done with some precision and coherence, according to the theological instincts of the new 'reformed Catholicism'

6 Gregory of Nyssa, 1995, 'On Virginity', in *Nicene and Post-Nicene Fathers of the Christian Church*, Second Series, vol. 5, translated by William Moore, Peabody, MA: Hendrickson, pp. 343–71, at p. 369.

of the Church in England in the sixteenth and seventeenth centuries. Throughout this early period of vernacular liturgical reform (and despite the various political and theological vicissitudes that marked the shifts between the early prayer books), the theology of vows remained shot through with a classically Augustinian theology of grace, and a deep sense thereby of the frailty of our human natures: the possibility of failure in vows, as too of restitution in them, was thus a core theme. The fundamental theology of baptism, however, was closely aligned to a theory of when and where a child should then proceed to a conscious further decision for Christ at confirmation and first Communion; the vows of marriage and ordination (no longer now mutually incompatible, of course, post-Reformation) were equally laid side by side in their potential overlap and new co-existence.

But the one sort of vow that was then no longer performed in the Church in England at the Reformation, of course, was that of *monastic* commitment. And hence the fascinating later political and ecclesiastical furores caused by their proposed re-introduction into national life in the aftermath of the Oxford movement in the nineteenth century, when new Religious communities were once again formed in Britain. As Petà Dunstan charts in Chapters 1 and 7, below, the consternation caused by this development at the level of parliament and Church was symbolically significant for the whole theory of vows, with which we continue to struggle. For the key issue then was the inevitable analogy between Religious vows and marriage vows, at a time when divorce was still staunchly disallowed by the Church of England. If *Religious* vows could fail, then, would not that then threaten also the entire 'erotic stability' of British marital life and society? The question continues to press in a new way today, even in our very different and supposedly liberal society, when the issue of homosexuality and marriage has now become the focus of greatest anxiety in the Anglican Communion; and we might say this crisis goes back to the heart of the paradox of allure and fear over vows, and their potential failures, with which we are dealing here throughout.

In short, any theology of *baptismal* vows has implications for the vowed life, all the way down (that is a basic presumption);

and the question of vows to the *Religious* life, specifically, has tended in the Anglican tradition to intensify analogous concerns about erotic stability in marriage and society, and concomitant questions about commitment and witness, poverty and wealth. It seems that these questions probe to a deeper level of thinking than we are now accustomed to about the ascetic project of virtue in our tradition as a whole. For we have been failing of late, we suggest, to think through the *radicality* of our historic tradition of vows; we have been performing them, to be sure, sometimes rather carelessly, but without sufficient attention to what we are *doing*.

It follows, therefore, that, as the chapters of this book unfold, certain further theses and proposals are unfurled to address our core questions, and our core paradox.

First, we suggest that the Church of England has, in recent decades, lamentably lost a *coherent* account of vows which would unite its various significant liturgical texts on vows, from baptism through confirmation, to marriage, ordination and indeed Religious vows (the last still being, however, *ad hoc* productions of each Religious community). All of these key liturgical texts have been altered *seriatim* in recent years, of course, sometimes more than once (before and in the era of *Common Worship*), to respond to pastoral pressures and a felt need to update and reform them in relation to contemporary life and language; but our supposition and concern is that this may have happened without a core, unified, theological sense of what vows connote at base, and how they can thus work to conjoin these various sacramental and liturgical manifestations. In particular, the liturgies of Anglican baptism have undergone more than one change in recent decades: first in the honourable direction of re-engaging all the profundity of ancient, lengthy and demanding rites of passage; and then, in somewhat timorous retreat from such, to a simpler and less exacting account of the baptismal transition, one deemed less confounding to the contemporary mind in baptism's (frankly disturbing) symbolism of death and life, drowning and rescue. We need hardly say, I hope, that members of the Littlemore Group – grounded as we are in the messy and complex realities of the parish – understand full well the pastoral exigencies of both sides of this liturgical argument about baptism. We continue to experience the profound spiritual challenges of how best to invite seekers, enquirers and even sceptical outsiders of every sort into the awe-inspiring rites of baptism.[7] But what we do want to ask, and ask afresh in this book, is what *theology of vows* now sustains the various liturgical texts of our tradition in which vows are called for, starting from baptism as the anchor of all other Christian vows: how do these relate to one another? Are these vows a life-and-death matter, or are they not? Do they make transcendent demands on those who make them, and how could those demands be newly expressed for our culture? Much that follows in this book seeks to re-address this problem in a creative but open spirit.

Secondly, we have come to the correlative view that the vows of confirmation, specifically, and indeed the importance of the sacrament of confirmation, are in danger within Anglicanism of becoming debased, or even covertly abandoned, *in favour of* baptism. And this issue too is strongly connected to one side of the core paradox of vows that we outlined above. If the great allure of the Christian life, and its accompanying vows, is closely connected with the *demands* that this life places upon us, then the period of adolescence or young adulthood is a particularly important one for reflection on these requirements and their transcendent meaning. While it is completely understandable that adult conversion and baptism would tend to trump any subsequent requirement of confirmation, that does not mean that confirmation should slip into the background of the Church's repertoire, or become merely the preserve of certain institutional captive audiences, such as private or Church schools. An adolescent *rite de passage* – akin to a *bar* (or *bath*) *mitzpah* in the Jewish tradition – may have immense spiritual power and significance at a transitional moment in religious and psychological growth into adulthood. It may indeed answer that need for transcendent seriousness and spiritual transformation about the Christian life that the attraction to new monasticism also raises in a parallel mode. We propose

7 For evidences of our response to these challenges, see Chapter 2, below, and Matthew Bullimore's chapter, 'Office: Baptism', in *For God's Sake*, pp. 47–61.

that the Church of England needs to think more, and think afresh, about confirmation and its sacramental significance.[8]

Thirdly, then, just as we see the various kind of Christian vows as inherently linked to one another, and founded unilaterally in baptism, so we have also come to see the life-long demands of (old) monastic life as importantly and creatively related to the various vows made by those in the parish, and *vice versa.* It is a distinctive feature of Anglican history that the recovery of the monastic/Religious life in the nineteenth century arose authentically out of urgent parish and missional exigences.[9] The new sisterhoods, especially, responded to poverty, sickness and educational needs in dauntingly self-sacrificial ways which at the same time were liberating for those sisters personally, and could now be called 'proto-feminist'; the male versions of these new experiments, also arising for the most part out of the parish, were often devoted to the poorest of the poor, and to areas in London, East Oxford and the new Northern industrial cities that even the police were sometimes afraid to enter. The very *offence* of restored monastic vows emerged, then, out of an *intensification* of baptismal and clerical vows which merely sharpened the focus of their deepest intent. As Fr Richard Meux Benson, founder of the Society of St John the Evangelist, was wont to stress, the Religious life was not something over and above the ordinary Christian life, but simply a proper return to what the ordinary Christian life should always have been, before the Church fell away from its true calling of being fully united with Christ.[10] In other words, it was in riposte to

8 See again, Chapter 3, below: Alex Hughes's discussion of confirmation there may interestingly be compared with Victoria Johnson's account of 'being beholden', in Chapter 11.

9 See again Petà Dunstan's contributions to this book: Chapters 1 and 7. To be sure, there were also some early romantic experiments in aestheticized versions of Anglican 'monasticism' that withdrew from the parish completely; but it is revealing that most of these did not last long. For a classic account of the origins and types of Anglican Religious life, see Anson, Peter F., 1955, *The Call of the Cloister*, London: SPCK. See also Frances Ward's exploration of the vulnerabilities of Anglican quasi-Religious community in Chapter 9, below.

10 The founding of the Society of St John the Evangelist (earlier named The Missionary Brotherhood) by Benson and two confrères in Oxford in 1865 is described in Anson's *The Call of the Cloister* (see n. 9), pp. 72–89. An extended history of the Society is now available in James, Serenhedd, 2019, *The Cowley*

the corrupted form of the Church of England – which Benson (and other Oxford Movement followers) disparagingly termed 'Christendom' – that the new Religious orders had their impetus, while remaining for and in that Church. Far from fleeing into a special Religious (or monastic) elitism, Benson saw his own new Religious movement as simply calling the Church back to its true self. And by the same token, such a risky venture could only be essayed because 'ordinary Christians' inspired and animated it in the first place. In other words, 'Religious' or 'monastic' renewal within Anglicanism *needed the parish just as much as the parish needed it*. This principle, we propose afresh in this book, is as important for Anglican Religious life as it ever was, and it also has very significant implications for the somewhat tricky relationship between old and new Anglican monasticisms today, which this book also charts.

Thus fourthly, and following from this last insight, a further argument emerges through this volume and its examination of the core paradox of the demands of a transcendent commitment, already outlined. And that is that the new monasticisms and the old monasticisms also need each other (as mutually inspiring, challenging and corrective phenomena), just as Anglican Religious life in general needs the parish, and *vice versa*. These two mutual needs are not coincidental, and are indeed themselves mutually entangled. As Ben Edson charts in some detail in Chapter 8, below, new monasticism can take many and different forms within the Anglican tradition, some primarily parish-based, some not. But with the perspective of some years of experimentation in mind, it is becoming clear that the staying-power of new monasticisms is often closely related to these groups' willingness to draw on at least some of the core, inherited, wisdom of the older monastic communities, just as some of these older monasticisms are finding themselves challenged and reinvigorated by the idealism, energy and missional boldness of the new.[11] Not that these relationships

Fathers: A History of the English Congregation of the Society of St John the Evangelist, Norwich: Canterbury Press.

11 We must note here the vital importance of the quiet and supportive presence of members of the French *Chemin Neuf* community in the St Anselm Community at Lambeth, stabilizing and guiding the younger members. Petà

are uncomplicated, of course, or without inevitable tensions: 'playing at monks' is a charge we have often heard levelled at the new monasticisms by sceptical members of the 'old' brigade, and the charge has indeed some point. Re-inventing the monastic wheel is not without its inevitable naïve fantasies and spiritual dangers, just as the new monastics can, in riposte, often quite easily point to areas of stuckness and rigidity in the older communities they encounter. The core nettle to be grasped, however, is that the vowed life is indeed *difficult*, all the way down; and no new community founded in a monastic spirit is going to avoid the raw agonies of an ongoing confrontation with human weakness and failure. But vows, we submit, are made precisely to confront this nexus of human weakness and failure, in God's grace and forgiveness, and not to flee from it.

And so too, and finally, this volume also points to the way in which the Church of England's tumultuous contemporary debates about sexuality, gender and *identity* are – and not coincidentally – also thrown up in this book repeatedly, as necessary accompanying topics in any serious reflection on the vowed life. For to confront the implications of any vow seriously is to probe precisely these matters: the question of our core identity before God in baptism; the issue of our erotic selfhood as drawn forth progressively in the processes of sanctification, whatever our vocation; the challenge of our frailty and honesty-before-God in bringing our sexual desire and quest for faithfulness into the orbit of divine love. All these pressing contemporary questions arise necessarily within the context of vows, as several chapters in this volume chart.[12] But it should

---

Dunstan makes some particularly searching comments on this same issue of the relation of 'old' and 'new' 'monasticisms' in Chapter 7, below.

12 See especially Chapters 2, 3, and 4, below. The Littlemore Group also remembers with gratitude a talk given to us by a senior Anglican Religious during the writing of this book, who underscored how complicated it has now become to be both gay and a Religious (whether 'out' or not); for whereas, as he put it, the Religious life was once the safest place to be a celibate homosexual, the new cultural scepticism about celibacy now makes it all the more difficult and seemingly unsafe. And yet celibacy lived well and faithfully can still act as a great encouragement to others, married or single, and whatever their identity or 'orientation'.

be noted that any *Christian* theology of vows also brings our current secular obsession with 'identity politics' under a certain judgement, not because there is no investment in the Church of England in finding justice and understanding for the previously voiceless, but because Christian vows presume and enact an identity *beyond* the merely individual. This is the one rooted in Christ at baptism, and located therefore in the solidarity of the Christian 'social' – 'the blessed company of all faithful people'. This is the mysterious, indeed mystical, reality of our Christian selfhood: irreducibly corporate, embodied, visible and active in the world. To believe and live into this reality, so that our often-frail sense of individual identity is fully affirmed, but at the same time taken up into something infinitely greater than we can 'ask or imagine', is at the heart of what our original baptismal vows both plead and enact.

It follows that, just as the parish needs the Religious life, and the old monasticism needs the new, so too – and within the perspective of all Christian vows-founded-in-baptism – we also need *each other* (married, unmarried, ordained, lay, or bound by Religious vows) in order to be held in faithfulness to Christ and to his Church. Put this way, monastic vows seem less like the *opposite* of marriage vows – let alone like some elite or higher calling – but rather are conjoined in a shared commitment and mutual witness, as demanding as the very sacrament of baptism itself.

In summary, then, and stemming from our core paradox of the simultaneous demand *for* and anxiety about the demand *of* vows, the essays below contribute some theological reflection on: the coherence of Anglican understandings of vows within liturgical practice and their sacramental context; the potential of renewing the practice of confirmation; what attention to the vowed life might offer to our ongoing conversations about sex, gender and identity; and on the benefits of what is now often called a 'mixed ecology' approach to the mutual dependence of the parish, traditional forms of monasticism, and the new monasticisms. Our hope is that they will unlock and free the *promise* of baptism – and the dependent forms of intensified vowed life – for the life of the Church.

In what follows, we dig a bit deeper to offer some clarification about exactly what a vow is, and especially how, in its Christian form, it is to be distinguished from a mere 'promise', or more importantly, from an 'oath'. And further, we probe more acutely what is distinctive about a Christian vow in relation to the problem of a *failure* in it. In our work together as a group, we found new light shed on this central matter from a slightly unexpected contemporary source, and a sceptical philosophical one, to boot. Sometimes a voice highly critical of Christianity can nonetheless uniquely focus the theological mind.

The Promise, the Oath, the Vow, and the Religious 'Form of Life'

There is surprisingly little contemporary theological literature about vows-in-general, we found. Indeed, most books about vows today tend to be about broken vows, whether they are Religious, marriage or ordination vows. Interestingly, it is a contemporary Italian linguistic and political philosopher, Giorgio Agamben (b. 1942), who has made discussion first of the nature of the oath, and then of Christian (vowed) monastic life, a key part of his critical philosophy.[13] We have found his reflections peculiarly generative for our own project, and we outline them briefly here, in order to bring our own theological proposals to a fit conclusion in response.

In his book, *The Sacrament of Language*, Agamben first discusses the purpose of oaths in the ancient world – oaths which might be said to be the *precursor* of Christian vows – and he does this in a revealing way. He cites the Roman statesman Cicero, who describes what an oath is, and what it obliges us to do, thus: 'An oath is an assurance backed by religious sanctity; and a solemn promise given, as before God as one's witness, is to be sacredly kept.' This obligation upon the one who makes the oath concerns justice and good faith – it is about *doing*

13 Agamben, Giorgio, 2011, *The Sacrament of Language: An Archaeology of the Oath*, translated by Adam Kotsko, Stanford, CA: Stanford University Press; and Agamben, Giorgio, 2013, *The Highest Poverty: Monastic Rules and Form-of-Life*, translated by Adam Kotsko, Stanford, CA: Stanford University Press.

what has been *promised*.[14] So an oath adds something very practical and public to a mere verbal promise.

Furthermore, Agamben notes that the ancient oath of the classical world was also seen as functioning to conserve and keep united a particular state of affairs. It was a way of confirming what was already the case – this is what Agamben calls an 'assertative oath'.[15] So, in this historical context, a person makes a solemn claim that something is true, or that something has happened, and promises that nothing will change. The oath confirms what is the case, and also guarantees that it will continue to be so, and so it has a 'promissory' aspect. Usually, the oath is sworn before the 'gods', as witnesses, or as those who offer a guarantee of the oath; or the oath is sworn in the name of *a* 'god', as if to provide faith in its efficacy. In fact, the swearing of the oath is an act of devotion, a self-consecration in which the person plights themselves to the 'gods' so they are under pain of vengeance should they renege on their word.

Agamben then pushes further, however, and argues that the idea of the oath is related to the divine in even a more fundamental way in the thought of the first-century Jewish philosopher, Philo (and this focus provides the transition into the linked, but deepened, concept of *vow*). In his allegorical writings on Gen. 22.16–17, Philo discusses the vow that God makes to Abraham when he establishes the covenant. Philo emphasizes that God swears *by himself*, writing: 'You mark that God swears not by some other thing, for nothing is higher than He, but by Himself, who is best of all things'.[16] Thus, while an oath might normally be sworn in the name of a God to assist *our* faith in it, God alone swears by *himself* as the one who is unchangingly faithful. Thus 'the very words of God are oaths', says Philo, because whatever God says, comes to pass. God is the truth in which word and action are one and God's word testifies with absolute certainty for itself. In God there is no fallibility, and so his words are true, and his promises are

14 See Cicero, *De officiis*, 3.29.10, cited in Agamben, *Sacrament of Language*, p. 3.

15 Agamben, *Sacrament of Language*, p. 6.

16 Philo, *Legum Allegoriae*, 204–8, quoted in Agamben, *Sacrament of Language*, p. 20.

fulfilled. Philo's belief that 'God spoke and it was done, with no interval between the two' chimes well, we can note, with Paul's later encouragement to the Thessalonians that God will bless them in this same way: 'The one who calls you is faithful, and *he will do it*' (1 Thess. 5.24).[17]

For Agamben, therefore, if a person makes an oath in the name of God it is almost as a *prayer*, for the person's words will be swept up into the truth and faithfulness of God; and this is where an oath tips into a *vow*. This special kind of oath (*qua* vow) is 'thus an attempt to conform human language to this divine model, making it as much as possible, *pistos*, credible.' Going further, Agamben then cites the Greek poet Aeschylus, to suggest that the vow is not so much that which adds credibility to a person, but that it is the person's adequation to the divine life that makes him or her believable: 'It is not the oath that makes us believe the man, but the man the oath' (Aeschylus, *Fragment 369*).[18] Or, in theological idiom, you do not trust me because I have made a vow but you trust my vow because of my prayerful desire that I might be Christlike in fulfilling it.

Agamben notes that this understanding of vow can be extended to all our speaking. To speak well, then, is a blessing, a bene-diction, in which we remain faithful to our word by our actions, and our actions give credence to our words. But to speak badly, in bad faith, is perjury, blasphemy and curse – a male-diction.[19] It is a word that has broken its truthful relation to things, and it is what constitutes us as fallen. Thus, as Agamben puts it more boldly and controversially, *all* our speech is in some sense a vow, in which we call upon God's aid to make good on our own word. As Augustine so artfully prayed: 'Thee do I invoke, God, Truth, in whom and by whom and through whom are all things true which are true'.[20]

But now we come to a central puzzle, which has to be confronted immediately by any Christian. For why is it that that

17 Philo, *De sacrificiis*, 65, quoted in Agamben, *Sacrament of Language*, p. 21.

18 Agamben, *Sacrament of Language*, p. 21–2.

19 Agamben, *Sacrament of Language*, p. 42.

20 Augustine, *Soliloquies*, 1.3, quoted in Agamben, *Sacrament of Language*, p. 57.

Jesus himself does not offer either an oath or a vow in his own teaching? Indeed, he seems to condemn the practice (see Matt. 5.33–7, to which we shall shortly return). In the light of the above analysis, there may be a ready answer for this problem. In Jesus, the *human* act of vowing is unnecessary, in that for him, as a divine Person (the second Person of the Trinity), his words and his actions are always one. There is no interval or discrepancy between them. In short, Jesus practises what he preaches and preaches what he practises. In Jesus the truth is witnessed in his 'form of life',[21] his way of living, his way of being in the world. He is the one who is the way, the truth and the life without remainder. So Christ does not himself vow, because his own word is always 'Yes': it is always the fulfilment of the divine promise. We see that all that he does is as a consummation of past promise, and as a pledge of promises yet to be fulfilled. In his saving death and his resurrection, in his inauguration of the kingdom and his pouring out of his Spirit on his body, the Church, he shows us his faithfulness by bestowing upon us a foretaste of our promised end with him.

If the Word of God is witnessed as a life lived, a living vow, so *our* human vows, our words, bind us to that Word. Our words should witness to our way of life, and our way of life should attest to the veracity of our words. Our word commits us to the 'form of life' that has been chosen for us by Christ, and which is, therefore, the life to which we are called and the life most fitting for us. We seek to align our words to the Word; our lives to his life. We bind ourselves to the truth in order that we may do the truth.

We can also now see why there is a prohibition against *human* oaths, or swearing in general, in the Gospels and in the Epistles (see again, Matt. 5.33–7; and James 5.12). An oath that would seek to add some guarantee to our human words and actions is prohibited insofar as that is rendered unnecessary if we are living a way of life that bears witness to the divine truth. The only thing necessary to add to a 'form of life' that is faithful and true is simply our assurance: our 'yes' and

21 Agamben uses Wittgenstein's rich but malleable notion of a 'form of life' as a key category in expounding the life of vows and Religious Rules.

our 'amen'.[22] Here is a demanding counsel of perfection, and it asks that our commitment to the one who is the truth should already be total. Our way of life should already be a refraction of his way of life.

However, we also know that we sin, that we constantly fall short of speaking the truth or of acting upon our word. Our lives signally fail to mirror Christ's way of life. And this is why the distinctively Christian vow is always and already in some sense *penitential* from the outset; for it recognizes our inevitable failures and our need to reaffirm that we will be gracefully aided in our speaking and doing. In other words, it is our underlying theology of grace that must also distinguish the Christian vow from any pagan oath, and indeed from any mere (private) promise. And this implies a distinctive doctrine of the *Spirit* for Christians. For while, as Agamben noted, ancient oaths and vows in general often called the 'gods' to be witnesses or guarantors of human words, in the Christian tradition, the supreme witness (or 'Advocate') is the Holy Spirit, the Person who witnesses and testifies to the love between the Father and the Son. The same Spirit is also that love made available to us and poured into our hearts (Rom. 5.5). In making a vow, then, the Christian calls upon the Spirit, the witness, in order that their life may itself be also a witness of that life-giving love through word and deed. And the vow of the fallen sinner is thus, by the same token, a confirmation of a grace already recognized, received and accepted *in* the Spirit; it is a commitment to live a way of life, to be in a certain way in the world, but it is also always an expression of our further and ongoing desire and need for grace and for forgiveness when we fail and once again have to repent and turn back into the Spirit's sanctifying embrace.

Of course, we want all of our speaking and doing to bear witness, in the Spirit, to the 'form' that is found uniquely in Christ. As Agamben also notes, this is all the more crucial when we see that we live in a world that is fearfully full of blasphemy – a world in which our speaking is uttered without reference

22 See Agamben, *Sacrament of Life*, p. 44.

to the truth, and our actions do not reflect our words.[23] A 'post-truth' world is one that is, in this sense, constitutively blasphemous. Our blasphemies are the words and actions that do *not* participate in God's faithfulness. They are empty and vain, and attest to a world that operates as if nothing is true, nothing matters, nothing has meaning. Nothing could be more different from a Christian vow, properly understood – in fact it is the antithesis of it.

In sum: Agamben has provided profound semantic and philosophical insights into promises, oaths and (Christian) vows – we might call this his layered phenomenological analysis of the palimpsest of different demands-before-God – which have inspired our theological reflections. Furthermore, his work on the 'sacrament of language' has also been enriched and complexified by his more recent work on the Religious life as such.[24] Given our interest in this book in charting the tight connection of Religious vows and other Christian vows, some of his apposite reflections here are also worth noting. We set out two clusters of reflection below, one starting from Agamben's analyses of monastic Rules, and the other from the side of the basic sacramental life of any Christian. The two closely interrelate.

First, then, Agamben seeks to clarify the intimate relationship between Religious vows and the practices demanded in the Rule of any formal Religious community. He begins by noting how a *saint's* life is rightly understood as re-performing the life of Christ in a new mode. He argues that the life of the saint actually provides the exemplary form of any Rule by which a Christian community should live. He cites Gregory Nazianzus, for instance, who in his *Oration 21*, described the life of St Anthony written by Athanasius as 'legislation for the monastic life in narrative form'.[25] In the life of the saint, he argues, we see how the monastic Rule becomes one with the life of

---

23 See Agamben, *Sacrament of Language*, pp. 40–2, 70–1.

24 Agamben, *The Highest Poverty* (see n. 13, above). It is ironic that this book is actually deeply critical of the monastic/Religious traditions it describes; but that does not invalidate its primary insights about the working of vows and of monastic 'Rules'.

25 Cited in Agamben, *The Highest Poverty*, p. 4.

the saint – it is a whole 'form of life' that witnesses to Christ. Agamben notes that in the Christian monastic life, therefore, the Rule should not be seen as an alien or imposed law, but through practice and habit it actually begins to coincide with a person's, and community's, way of life. In such a way, it forms a whole *new* 'form of life' in which the Rule and life become one. He notes how this habituation is taken quite literally to name the vesture of the Religious – the 'habit'.[26] The form of life becomes, under grace, 'habitual' – a way that the self is constituted through practice and relationships. It becomes, in other words, a 'dwelling': something inhabited or 'put on'. Already in Col. 3.12–17, we might note, the Pauline writer there speaks of the need to be 'clothed' with virtues, and most of all to be 'clothed in love'. He encourages us to a way of life that becomes as fitting to us as our favourite clothes, or even a second skin; and this anticipatorily evokes the monastic 'habit', with all its symbolic overtones.[27]

It follows, therefore, that every vow marks a commitment to a *practice*, one that entails an implicit *Rule* of life; but the Rule that is followed then needs over time to become internalized, *habitual*, and etched into one's life as a whole. This recalls Paul's early exhortation to a work of unceasing prayer (1 Thess. 5.17): the whole of life, its hours punctuated with formal worship, becomes a prayer, an offering, a conforming of oneself to Christ's life through this particular mode of Christian living. In this way the whole of life becomes a *divine* work (such as George Herbert who, in the later Anglican tradition, expressed this so well in his poetry and other writings[28]): life is sanctified overall, and the self-in-community is conformed to the model, the exemplar, the 'form', of Christ.

Note then that this side of Agamben's analysis of vows and Rules in the Religious life intimates its significance for the life of Christians more generally, even if they are not technically

26 Agamben, *The Highest Poverty*, pp. 13–16.

27 Further reflections on the significance of Religious dress are found in Sr Judith's chapter, 6, below.

28 See especially, for Herbert's theological and poetic legacy, Carrigan, Henry L., Jr. (ed.), 2021, *The Temple: The Poetry of George Herbert (Christian Classic)*, Brewster, MA: Paraclete Press. *The Temple* originated in 1633.

bound by a formal Rule. And so we come to a second related reflection. For it is possible to extend these considerations of the life of the Religious to every Christian life: it is in the vows of baptism, as we too have already argued above, that an implicit Rule (or form) of life emerges which, if fully heeded, leads to a conforming of oneself to Christ. The old self is stripped off so that a new self, a new 'form of life', is lived (see Rom. 6.5–10; Col. 3.9–10). This Rule of life issues from the 'form of life' that is Christ's own life, made manifest in his multi-faceted body, the Church. This principle, then, should apply no less to the non-Religious, parish-based, 'form of life' as to the Religious. But it is not inappropriate, we suggest, when such a longing for Christ's 'form of life' is divested of all romantic fantasy or false projection, for those in parish life to seek *in* the Religious presence within Anglicanism a continual and intensified reminder of, and aspiration towards, this fundamental Christian goal. Once again, the parish and the Religious life may mutually interact and support one another, if the fundamental meaning of Christian vows is well understood.

These final conclusions, it should be said, go well beyond what Agamben himself explicitly proposes; for he himself has remained a renowned sceptic about the long-term value of the Christian Religious life, despite all his penetrating insights into its origins and impetus. It remains, then, an irony and an object-lesson, that a European post-modern political philosopher of such standing – one profoundly influenced by towering non-Christian thinkers such as Wittgenstein and Foucault – could simultaneously illuminate the phenomenon of Religious vows with such renewed insight, and at the same time pour sceptical criticism on the history of Christian religious communities as they have developed over time.

But is this not yet another manifestation of the core paradox with which we started? Perhaps in the matter of Christian vows, properly understood, that allure and revulsion will always coexist as understandable human responses. The deeper question, of course, is what *God* wants of us in the axis of this paradox, the axis of Christian vows themselves. And this is what this volume is about.

Some Conclusions, as this Book Unfolds

Let us then draw some final conclusions to this Introduction.

In his remarkable little book, *Nomad of the Spirit: Reflections of a Young Monastic*,[29] the former Cistercian Bernardin Schellenberger muses memorably on what he calls the 'romantic misunderstanding' of a monk's life as a kind of 'ornamental hermit'. He tells the story of a strange kind of 'profession' that emerged in the later eighteenth and nineteenth centuries, in both England and Germany: that of becoming a paid 'anchorite' to decorate the extended gardens of large estates, and so to suggest to the owners and visitors (who also sometimes dressed up as 'monks') that something spiritual and exotic was still being effected in these confected 'wildernesses' and parks of the privileged. (Unfortunately, it turns out that at least some of these hired 'monastics' got fired expeditiously for sneaking off on a regular basis to the pub.) Schellenberger's further claim – perhaps more speculative – is that these fantasy 'monks', all too unreliable in their ascetic consistency, then got replaced by carved wooden replicas hidden among the trees and bushes, thus paving the way for modern, suburban, garden *gnomes*, with all their colourful allure – and doubtful aesthetic tastefulness! The genealogy is intriguing, if curious. But the spiritual lesson is pointed: we moderns (and post-moderns) still suffer from certain fantasies about the monastic life, says Schellenberger, certain 'wishes, dreams, yearnings and illusions', which for those who entertain such projections, they 'would never seriously follow in shaping their own lives'. For such romantic projections, he says, could only 'be realized, at best, by stuffed or painted hermits'.[30]

It has been the burden of this Introduction to explore how our contemporary life, both secular and Christian, is still seemingly haunted by the 'ornamental hermit' fantasy; and yet at the same time to show how something much more profound lurks underneath: that even greater yearning for the 'interesting thing' which is *God*. It is the concern of the chapters that follow

29 Schellenberger, Bernardin, 1981, *Nomad of the Spirit: Reflections of a Young Monastic*, London: Sheed and Ward.

30 *Nomad of the Spirit*, p. 16.

to help us re-imagine the costliness and joy of Christian vows, to re-conceive their interrelation, and to reassert and explore the significance of the monastic form of vows for the renewal of our Church today. For it is not more garden gnomes that we need, however charming and quirky, but rather, as Gregory of Nyssa put it, living, breathing examples of vows well-lived; for 'Any theory divorced from living examples ... is like [an] unbreathing statue'.[31] We hope and pray that this book, offered like all the Littlemore Group's work for the reflection of the Church at large, will stimulate thinking, prayer and renewed commitment in the matter of *The Vowed Life*. For, we believe, it is in submitting ourselves to the *demand* of baptism – and its concomitant forms of vowed life – that we will open ourselves more fully to the *promise* of baptism: the blessing that comes when our lives are conformed to the One who is faithful.

31 See again, Gregory of Nyssa, 'On Virginity' (n. 6, above), at p. 368.

PART I

Re-Thinking Anglican Vows: The Integrity of Vows in the Christian Life

I

The Revival of the Religious Life in the Church of England: How Vows Became Newly Contentious in a Victorian Culture of Convention

PETÀ DUNSTAN

In this chapter, which provides historical orientation for all that follows in this book, Petà Dunstan traces the developments in nineteenth-century Anglicanism out of which a revival in Religious life emerged and became contentious – on account of its vows. The responses to this renewal of Religious life were, to be sure, complex and paradoxical: a fear of 'popery' animated one critique; a resistance to (proto)-feminism, as represented by the new women's Religious orders, represented another sort of cultural anxiety; but a further (and core) factor concerned celibate Religious vows as potentially threatening to married life but also imitative of its desired erotic permanence – a token thereby of social transformation, political solidarity and identification with the poor. Such a vocation could not therefore be merely *personal. In short, the new 'vowed life' helped expose Victorian social inequalities and ultimately contributed effectively to national reform – educational, social, political and economic. It also raised afresh the whole question of what vows bespeak, in the Church of England and for the wider culture.*

The industrial revolution in the early nineteenth century and the accompanying population growth changed urban parish life in Britain irrevocably. Vicars in major towns saw their parishes transformed by smoke-producing factories and hastily built tenement blocks to house the workers, who had been recruited from the countryside. The accommodation was basic, with little provision for adequate sanitation. The air was polluted. Over-crowding, disease and misery followed. Local parish priests were powerless to stop the growth, and yet they were expected to cope with the social problems and spiritual challenges it brought.

The response had to be an increase both in the provision of churches and of clergy. The government responded with a series of large financial grants to build new churches, but this did not touch the social or educational problems.[1] By 1840 it was clear also that extra curates alone could not meet the pastoral demand. Many clergy began to see the need for additional dedicated parish workers. A revival of Religious orders would be one way of supplying the need, particularly for female workers who might more easily reach the women and children of the parish than a male vicar might do. The Lutherans in Germany had a deaconess community based at Kaiserworth (founded 1836); why, they thought, could the Church of England not found something similar?

The Tractarian movement in Oxford from 1833 provided an intellectual and theological justification for the same call. The movement began as a counter to liberal ideas both in contemporary political and theological debates. In seeking an alternative to the prevailing trends, the Tractarians looked back to the Patristic period for theological inspiration and as the source for renewal of the Church of England. Here they found theology was embedded in a monastic culture, and the lack of Anglican Religious communities therefore became a source of concern for them. It would be one of the Tractarian leaders, Edward Pusey, who encouraged Marian Hughes to be the first woman to take vows (1841) in the Church of England since the dissolution of the monasteries. Pusey also was signifi-

1 A bill to provide universal education for children had to wait until 1870. An act to bring standards to the building of homes did not pass until 1875. The provision of sewerage systems began only in the mid-nineteenth century, with London leading the way, 1859–65.

cant in the founding of the first community in Park Village, London, in 1845.

The social demands and the theological impetus together led various parish priests to explore creating women's communities in their districts. John Mason Neale in Sussex, Thomas T. Carter in Clewer, near Windsor, William Butler in Wantage and John Sharp in Horbury[2] were some of the most well-known. Some foundations faded quickly as the inexperience in Religious life of both the participants and their spiritual guides proved injurious. But others, such as those founded by the priests named above, survived the challenges and began to flourish with many recruits. The range of ministries that the communities tackled was wide: schools, hospitals, orphanages and refuges were established, while other Religious laboured in parishes, from running Sunday schools to visiting the sick and elderly.

The founding of men's communities was more complex, for men already had an outlet for parish ministry – they could seek ordination. Bishops were reluctant to allow those with a vocation to the priesthood to be (from an episcopal point of view) 'side-lined' into community life. Communities for men were established in the second half of the nineteenth century, but the early years of the revival of Religious life was focused on women. The veiled (proto-)feminist dimension of this development may now, with the benefit of hindsight, be the more apparent.

There was, however, plenty of initial hostility. The political prejudice against Roman Catholicism – the religion of Britain's major enemies for several centuries – meant that any echo of 'popery' within the Church of England aroused fear in many parishioners. Given that there was rioting in some places merely over a vicar wearing a surplice, groups of Anglican women in monastic-style habits were a provocation to certain sections of opinion. Anglican sisters were derided and threatened in numerous locations. That Religious communities were also associated with greater ritual in worship

2 Neale founded the Society of St Margaret (1855), Carter the Community of St John Baptist (1852), Butler the Community of St Mary the Virgin (1848), and Sharp the Community of St Peter (1858).

also hampered acceptance. Convent chapels were suspected of 'Romish' practices. The climate of suspicion made advocating for the Religious life hazardous, but it also meant that trying a vocation became 'counter-cultural', even dangerous, and therefore a radical and defiant path for those who wanted to protest against the growing economic, educational and social deprivations of Victorian society. The very idea, then, of Religious communities among Anglicans was a challenge that became a controversy.

It was only as years passed, therefore, and the sacrificial service of Religious was appreciated, whether as nurses fearlessly visiting the sick amidst cholera and typhoid epidemics at home, or nursing military personnel overseas in the Crimean war, that majority opinion shifted. *Punch* cartoons in the 1860s still mocked women dressing in habits but not the work they did. As the 1878 Report on Sisterhoods and deaconesses put it:

> In our own Church it is most certain that since sisterhoods have been revived ... the value of the work which they have done can hardly be overstated ... [T]hey have earned a character for usefulness which we believe scarcely any one (however opposed to them in principle) would venture to question.[3]

The acceptance through social works had the knock-on effect, however, of making those called to a more contemplative way of life in prayer hide their vocation. Communities called particularly and exclusively to a cloistered life did not emerge until the early twentieth century.

From the bishops, there was a general welcome for the ministry of women Religious. However, the problem for them was the issue of vows. For a Religious, taking vows in a community was an extension of the baptismal vows, a working out of the promises made when they became members of the Church. They were akin to marriage vows, sacramental in intention even if not seen as such by the Church. They wanted bishops to receive and sanction them. Yet to the bishops this created both

3 Page 5 of the text of the report attached to the 1878 *Chronicle of Convocation* (Canterbury), London: Rivingtons.

a theological and a political headache. If the vows were private promises, they were nothing to do with the bishops; but if they were on a par with marriage vows, then there had to be rules and regulations regarding those who might break them. There was not even civil divorce (except by Act of Parliament) until 1857, so if Religious vows were similar, they too were indissoluble. Formal acceptance of Religious vows therefore might well require passing canon law to govern them. This whole thorny issue rumbled on for years and is discussed more fully in a later chapter (Chapter 7, below). However, this controversy was why the vowed life was not simply about communities, but about the wider challenge of vows as a whole within the Church.

From the parish perspective, the emergence of Religious communities was more of a success than not. Some vicars saw the women Religious as their 'parish workers', and they held authority over them via their role as Warden. Traditionally, communities required a priest to be the overall leader and so, as ordination was not then open to women, female communities needed a male priest as the Warden. In these cases, while the mother or sister-in-charge ruled the community indoors, the ordering of the chapel and the priorities for the parochial work remained the decisions of the vicar. In later decades, some mother superiors shrugged off this outside authority but in the early years it served as a way of linking the community into local pastoral work and providing a shield of ecclesiastical protection against critics. The volume of work assumed also made it hard for opponents, for they usually were in favour of the particular ministry and its achievements – and if the nuns were banished the work would collapse. Therefore, opposition based on prior social prejudice began to dissolve except among ardent anti-Catholics whose grounds were theological. These theological opponents became outnumbered by those who supported the communities generously with funds for buildings and outreach, regarding the community ministries as charity work worthy of support.

The potent witness of communities' works was especially clear in the institutions they founded. Schools and hospitals for the poor, orphanages and refuges for women in trouble, were all a challenge to the state authorities, revealing the lack of universal provision. The response from the government came first in education, when the 1870 Education Act provided for the setting up of schools wherever local churches and charities (including communities) had not yet managed to build. After 1944, many church schools were absorbed into the state system. In nursing, it was the Nursing Sisters of St John the Divine who had provided Florence Nightingale with some of her training and their hospitals provided the route for the establishment of nursing as a profession, including district nurses as well as those working in hospitals.[4] One of the NSSJD sisters campaigned for the registration of midwives, leading to the 1902 Act. By the 1920s, the state had provided ways to train as a nurse (SRNs) without the need to go via a community and its institutions. Such examples were a sign of the success of Religious communities, yet at the same time sowing seeds for the decline in the number of sisters. Once the state provided social services, the community contribution was less needed and vocations to the professions were decoupled from Religious life itself.

However, in the early years of the revival of Religious communities, they were the pioneers and their achievements attracted further recruits. For many upper- and middle-class Victorian women, imprisoned in social expectations of delicacy and an ornamental life, restricted to activity in the home or chaperoned when in public, the life of a nun was a chance to work for social renewal as well as fulfil their spiritual life. It combined a freedom from the social norms with a chance to minister, to create and sometimes to lead in the struggle for a better life for the under-privileged. While for working-class women, most with the prospect only of combining domestic drudgery with the grind of regular childbearing, the convent could be a haven, a chance to gain education and a place to find confidence in achievement. The vowed life was not a restrictive one, then, but one that freed the person to use their gifts. Equally of significance was that many Victorian women were

4 Helmstadter, Carol and Godden, Judith, 2011, *Nursing before Nightingale 1815–1899*, London: Ashgate.

infused with a religious spirit, and in a community they could delve deeper into their spiritual side.

The decline in the number of vocations to the Religious life among Anglicans began at the First World War (1914–18). Some communities did continue to grow even as late as the 1960s, such as the Franciscans (SSF), but these were the exception. A women's community like the Community of St John Baptist had around 300 sisters in 1914, a number which fell to 200 by 1939, and to 100 in 1959. The greater opportunities for women in the professions and the workplace were part of the change, as well as the slow yet steady decline in religious affiliation through the twentieth century. The same fall in vocations was manifest in the Roman Catholic Church in the post-Second World War period, and this led to the Second Vatican Council (1962–66) producing a document on the renewal of the consecrated life. This development affected Anglican Religious as they too struggled with the decline in vocations and the demise of their institutions.

The main call was to return to the founder's charism. The difficulty for Anglicans (unless they were Benedictines or Franciscans looking back to the wider founders of their movement rather than the specific community) was that Anglican founders were high Victorians, steeped in neo-gothic sensibility and the romantic movement. Yet, this was exactly the inheritance that many in the mid-twentieth century were trying to banish. Anglican communities' attempts to modernize often caused anguish within and without their houses – and neither those orders who pursued a radical path, nor those who refused to change customs or outlook, were saved from the decline. By the 1960s several social and religious trends had accelerated to the extent that Religious were left looking old-fashioned and no longer relevant.

As communities shrank in numbers, Religious began to be seen less and less in parishes. Ordained Religious running parishes were a mere handful in number. Women Religious who had been the mainstay of many a Sunday school or sacristy withdrew as the older sisters retired and there were none to replace them. For example, for decades veiled sisters occupied several rows of seats at the front of the congregation at Our Most Holy Redeemer, Clerkenwell, at Sunday Mass, the Bethany nuns walking in orderly formation from their Lloyd Square convent nearby. A few nuns were directly on hand to serve the church in cleaning, mending and running children's activities. The presence of the sisters had encouraged vocations to the Religious life, including one future Benedictine abbot. By 1971, however, they were gone, the numerically reduced community of sisters having relocated to the south coast. This pattern of withdrawal was repeated in many Catholic-minded parishes. The celibate vowed life was no longer so visible. The habited nuns when seen were viewed as something from a previous generation, while those who had donned ordinary clothes no longer seemed to be distinct from any other social workers.

In the latter part of the twentieth century, a sense of doubt and despair undermined the communities' confidence. Those who had entered a large vibrant community did not know how to cope in a frailer, older context. The large buildings were no longer an inspiration but a financial burden, unsuitable for older sisters trying to care for the even older seniors. Yet the new houses they moved to could seem more like residential homes than convents, with so few younger members. Other communities divided into small groups in scattered branch houses, where community activities were reduced to a minimum and it was difficult for anyone new to join. Emotionally, there was some anger and self-criticism and much bewilderment. But the Religious had been caught in a whirlwind not of their own making. They did not realize at the time, but their role was to survive the winter season not embrace despair for the summer that was gone.

The one area in the 1970s and beyond where interest in Religious life grew was in the wider 'family' of the communities. Some Benedictine communities had oblates, the Franciscans had a Third Order, others had associates. These groups had existed for many decades. Indeed the first Franciscan tertiaries and Benedictine oblates among Anglicans emerged in the nineteenth century. The 1878 Report on sisterhoods noted:

> [T]here are many ladies who work as associates, some of whom reside for a considerable part of the year with the sisters in houses belonging to the communities.[5]

Post-1945, this group gradually grew in number and significance, living a modifed Rule of the community in what otherwise was a secular life. The members could marry and have families and had to provide for themselves economically, but they would make promises after a period of formation that linked them to the original community. The most spectacular growth came with the Third Order of the Society of St Francis (TSSF) which grew to nearly 2,000 members by the late twentieth century. These non-celibate Religious were witnessing directly in their parish churches, and some clergy too became members.

The Advisory Council, set up in 1935 to have a gentle oversight of Religious communities, and which included bishops as well as representatives elected from among the professed Religious, introduced a path of 'acknowledgement' for these communities. The celibate communities are 'recognized', the non-celibate 'acknowledged'. Both are regarded as legitimate expressions of the call to Religious life and the move has provided an encouragement for new experiments in community life.

Since the 1990s, there has been the emergence of what are popularly known as 'new monasticisms'.[6] These are expressions of Christian community, some attached to parishes, others evolving as extra-parochial. They can consist of family groups including children sharing a common life, or can concentrate on younger single people or another combination. Some are residential, others are dispersed. They have emerged from different strands of Anglicanism and some are consciously ecumenical. Indeed, there are a few groups that include non-Christians as well as Christians. What unites them all is a desire for prayer and a sharing of time and resources as a basis for exploring a Christian commitment. As already discussed in the Introduction

5 Page 6 of the text of the report attached to the 1878 *Chronicle of Convocation* (Canterbury).

6 Manifestations of these new 'monastic' movements are discussed throughout this book, but especially in Chapter 8, below.

to this volume, the current Archbishop of Canterbury, Justin Welby, has recognized the power of this movement of the spirit and seen it as an essential part of the renewal of the whole Church. He called a meeting of representatives of many of the new groups with the recognized communities at Lambeth Palace in March 2014 to encourage the phenomenon. Some of the new communities have faded, others are evolving. This is an echo of the original revival which was varied and changeable and unpredictable. However, from the development has emerged an excitement about the possibilities of Religious life for the twenty-first century.

The newer groups face challenges – when and how to write a Rule of Life, how to choose leaders, how to relate to the local parish, whether to introduce vows – and all these questions being asked in the context of being seen by some as a new hope for the revival of the Church as well as of Religious life. This expectation can be a burden when internal community structures have yet to be settled. The relationship to the more traditional celibate communities is also a question, for the new groups are not usually 'monastic' in the established sense of the word, and it can be complicated for new forms of community to adopt the ancient nomenclature of abbots and mother superiors, vows and profession, and distinct forms of dress. Some new groups do borrow from established customs and some do not, but how much to connect with the tradition is an ongoing question. That is because grafting 'monastic' patterns and terms onto an evolving community can distort as well as support a new venture. It can create a feeling of inferiority among members when in contact with established celibate Religious. However, the increased contact between 'recognized' and 'acknowledged' has helped dismantle some anxieties on both sides.

But what of the recognized communities? While some have faded away, others have survived the chill winds of secularism. The intense and particular call of the 'recognized' Religious life is a challenge and encouragement to looser community elsewhere, and so its survival is a significant part of the Archbishop of Canterbury's call to renew communities of prayer and service at the heart of the Church. This is a call to all types of community, reflecting the importance of a rhythm of prayer and a commitment to shared values that infuses the charism of Religious life. So will the established communities and new communities survive?

Looking back on the nineteenth century, communities that survived were those who developed a deep sense of *purpose*. This stemmed from strong spiritual values coupled with defined ministries and areas of witness. The communities that flourished were also those who attracted vocations from those able to lead – neither dictatorially nor quixotically – with an ability to articulate the shared vision. The ability to look outwards to society was significant, as communities could implode if they become too preoccupied with internal issues; even contemplative cloistered Religious have thrived best when aware of the world to which they witness through prayer. The problem has been the necessity to be connected to those in need of ministry at the same time as avoiding outside interference. Some Anglican communities deliberately chose to be extra-parochial in the nineteenth century to avoid domineering vicars and bishops. In doing so, they came to depend on a select group of sympathetic Anglo-catholic parish clergy to channel vocations to them, and when that group suffered decline in the wake of the social changes that accelerated after the Second World War (1939–45), they had lost their main source of new life. Religious life can attract recruits from many different parts of the Church, but the close identification of some communities with specific groups proved damaging when the ecclesiastical landscape changed. Religious life was associated for some with 'old-fashioned' practices and views, and was discarded along with maniples and humeral veils and certain rituals. Instead of being a witness to the faith, it was seen as an accessory, relevant in a previous age but now redundant and to be left to fade. Other communities that remained visible in the parish system, whether through missions or a more settled presence, such as the Society of St Francis (SSF), were able to connect with potential candidates for the novitiate more readily, and therefore attracted vocations in the 1970s and 1980s against the trend elsewhere. Such communities have also declined numerically overall but they have survived and even regenerated of late.

The link with parishes therefore has a role in the revival of Religious life. Parishes can nurture faith and vocations. They can provide outlets for evangelization, ministries and outreach for communities. They can be the place of contact between those with a call to service and the Religious communities of all types. However, the temptation in the past decades has been to point those with a call to serve the Church towards the path of ordination, without the opportunity to explore Religious life, either as an alternative or as an additional element to that call.

This situation is beginning to change because the significance of the presence of the vowed life in the Church can be seen more clearly. The vows Religious take cannot be subsumed in social custom. In the popular mind, baptism can be seen as a 'rite of passage', an excuse for a family party, instead of a solemn undertaking. Marriage vows in contemporary society can be diluted by the commercial pressures of weddings and the sense of easy dissolution if the two people wish to 'move on'. Even ordination can seem to outsiders as a route to a role in society, a job, a living, instead of a vocation, a promise to God. But the vows of Religious cannot be so diluted or explained away. They are an unequivocal challenge to a secular and agnostic society, what some have named the 'ultimate wager on God'. Their seriousness and implications are a witness both inside and outside the Church. They call us back to the seriousness of the other vows Christians take. This is why the Religious life in the Church is of such particular value.

It is the task of the rest of this book to unfold the relationship of all vows in the Church to the primary vows of baptism, and then to reflect afresh on how Religious vows, especially, sharpen the significance of those in contemporary culture.

But where are the 'pinch-points' in Anglican practices of baptism today? To this question we now turn.

2

'Name this child': Speech, Identity and Life-long Commitment in Baptismal Vows

JOEL LOVE

In this chapter on the fundamental nature of baptismal vows, Joel Love starts from a contemporary conundrum about gender identity, and works back from there to re-explore the uniqueness of a vow which hands over our human personhood into the mystical (and corporate) body of Christ for ever. 'The vowed life' is thus always at root the life of our baptismal vows, even though others often originally make these vows for *us. And thus any renewal in a theology of vows, more generally, must inexorably start with a renewal of the theology of baptism.*

'God knows each of us by name and we are his.'[1]

During my curacy, my training incumbent was approached by a female-to-male trans person with a request to be 're-baptized'. He was worried that God did not know him by his new name, since he had been baptized as a child with a girl's name. My incumbent asked me how I thought we should respond, and it seemed clear to me that the Bible was unequivocal when it says: 'There is one body and one Spirit, just as you were called to the one hope of your calling, one Lord, one faith, *one baptism*, one

1 2015, *Common Worship Christian Initiation: Additional Baptism Texts in Accessible Language*, London: Church House Publishing: www.churchofengland.org/prayer-and-worship/worship-texts-and-resources/common-worship/christian-initiation/holy-baptism-5 (accessed 21 November 2022).

God and Father of all, who is above all and through all and in all' (Eph. 4.4–5, emphasis mine). There can be no re-baptism. A so-called 'provisional' baptism – while possible – would only have sown doubt and confusion about whether God had ever been with this person on his journey.

The underlying theological point is that for Christians, their most fundamental identity is *in Christ*. This is a consistent theme in the New Testament epistles (see, for example, 2 Cor. 5.17: 'if anyone is in Christ, there is a new creation: everything old has passed away; see, everything has become new!'). The House of Bishops' report which has reiterated this point[2] continues with this qualification: 'But that does not mean that all the other identities which people bring to Christ are marginal or unimportant' (paragraph 76). This man's request for re-baptism was really a question about identity, and this chapter will be an exploration of the link between vows, names, and identity. Through this, it will also be possible to underscore afresh the foundational demand and commitment of baptism.

With regard to the actual person in the parish who raised the searching question about baptism and identity, we responded by offering him the opportunity to re-affirm his baptismal vows and sign himself with water from the font in a public ceremony in the presence of God and of his loved ones, and in his new name.[3] Baptism is the sacrament of new birth, and is therefore linked in deeply physical and spiritual ways to the question of

---

2 The Pilling Report, compiled by the House of Bishops Working Group on Human Sexuality and chaired by Sir Joseph Pilling, was published by Church House Publishing on 28 November 2013.

3 The General Synod of the Church of England subsequently declared in July 2017: 'That this Synod, recognizing the need for transgender people to be welcomed and affirmed in their parish church, call on the House of Bishops to consider whether some nationally commended liturgical materials might be prepared to mark a person's gender transition' (GS 2071A). According to the Church of England website, the House of Bishops has prayerfully considered whether such a service is indeed required. The Bishops decided that it was not. Instead, they are inviting clergy to use the existing rite *Affirmation of Baptismal Faith*, for which new guidance is also being prepared: https://www.churchofengland.org/more/media-centre/news/services-mark-gender-transition-house-bishops-response (accessed on 5 February 2022). Gender identity is featured throughout the Church of England's recent discussion document *Living in Love and Faith*: https://www.churchofengland.org/sites/default/files/2020-11/LLF%20Web%20Version%20Full%20Final.pdf (accessed 5 February 2022).

identity (recall the biblical trope of being 'known' or 'called' while still in the womb, as at Jer. 1.5 or Ps. 139). Baptismal identity, being baptized 'into Christ', is a deeper identity than all other identities because it defines us first, prior to any other identity that we may inhabit: 'As many of you as were baptized into Christ have clothed yourselves with Christ. There is no longer Jew or Greek, there is no longer slave or free, there is no longer male and female; for all of you are one in Christ Jesus' (Gal. 3.27–28). We note also that baptism makes us 'one'. It is a shared identity, not an individual one. And in relation to gender, our baptismal identity 'in Christ' is more important than whether we are male or female (or both, or neither).[4] In this chapter, I will argue that true, baptismal identity is not something that we possess or create, but rather an eschatological reality that we only discover gradually or towards which we find ourselves being 'called'.

In *For God's Sake* (an earlier Littlemore Group publication), Matthew Bullimore has teased out the many layers of meaning in Christ's baptism by John, and in the baptism 'with the Holy Spirit and fire' (Luke 3.16).[5] None of these baptisms are specifically 'naming' ceremonies in the sense in which most twenty-first century people understand them. Yet the practice of naming a child at their baptism does recognize the linked themes of identity, community, and eschatology that are present in New Testament descriptions of baptism. Though the naming of Jesus takes place in Matt. 1.25, it is at his baptism that his identity is revealed: 'And a voice from heaven said, "This is my Son, the Beloved, with whom I am well pleased"' (Matt. 3.17). Likewise, when human beings are baptized their identity is joined with that of Jesus Christ, specifically in his death and resurrection. Baptism thus anticipates the eschaton and allows us to participate in the realities that will obtain at the end of time.

---

4 See, for example, the summary of recent work on baptismal identity in Cheng, Patrick S., 2011, *Radical Love: An Introduction to Queer Theology*, New York: Seabury, p. 120.

5 See Bullimore, Matthew, 2016, 'Office: Baptism', in Martin, Jessica and Coakley, Sarah (eds), *For God's Sake: Re-Imagining Priesthood and Prayer in a Changing Church*, Norwich: Canterbury Press, pp. 47–61, esp. pp. 50–5.

The only 'name' that the Bible associates with baptism is the name of the Father and of the Son and of the Holy Spirit. It is the name 'in' which Jesus says that new disciples should be baptized (Matt. 28.19). This is because all sacraments begin with God's grace and then include us in what God is already doing. The words spoken at baptism (the 'vows') are our response to God's prior 'Word' (or promise) to us.[6] In this exchange of vows, from God to us and from us to God, the sacrament of baptism resembles a covenant. As such, baptism dramatizes the experience of conversion in a way that is both individual and corporate. The prior promise of God comes through very clearly in the *Book of Common Prayer* (and in similar words in the proposed 1928 revision), where 'Ye have heard also that our Lord Jesus Christ hath promised in his holy Word, to grant all those things that we have prayed for; which promise he, for his part, will most surely keep and perform'. It is on this basis that those who come to be baptized must also make promises in return. In the 'Publick Baptism of Infants', 'this Infant must also faithfully, for his part, promise by you that are his sureties (until he come of age to take it upon himself), that he will renounce the devil and all his works, and constantly believe God's holy Word, and obediently keep his commandments'. In the Baptism of 'such as are of riper years', the same promises are made 'in the presence of these your witnesses, and this whole Congregation'. There is no getting away from the public and corporate nature of the baptismal vows, nor from their profound and demanding seriousness.

Parents and godparents make vows 'for' or 'on behalf of' the child. This is a vicarious action. However, baptism liturgies always anticipate a future moment when the child will find his or her own voice in order to affirm their vows, thereby becoming further integrated into the community of speech but importantly not independent of it. This much is clear from 'The Order of Confirmation or laying on of hands upon those that

6 Understood both as a promise offered to us, and as an invitation to further conversation (both ideas are present in the 'λόγος' of John 1.1). See O'Rourke Boyle, Marjorie, 2006, 'A Conversational Opener: The Rhetorical Paradigm of John 1.1' in Jost, Walter (ed.), *A Companion to Rhetoric and Rhetorical Criticism*, Oxford: Wily-Blackwell, pp. 58–79.

are baptized and come to years of discretion' in the *Book of Common Prayer*. The candidates for confirmation affirm the vows made on their behalf at their baptism: 'Do ye here, in the presence of God, and of this Congregation, renew the solemn promise and vow that was made *in your name* at your Baptism; ratifying and confirming the same in your own persons, and acknowledging yourselves bound to believe and to do all those things, which your Godfathers and Godmothers then undertook for you?'[7] Note the phrase 'in your name' (emphasis mine), to which we will return below.

It should be noted, however, that the exact wording and status of baptismal vows has changed over time. The *Alternative Service Book* (1980) spelled out the link between baptism and confirmation a little differently: godparents must be 'willing' (strictly speaking this is not a vow) to 'help' the child learn 'to be faithful in public worship and private prayer, to live by trust in God, and come to confirmation'. There is a return to the specific language of vows in *Common Worship* (2000), where parents and godparents vow to 'pray', to 'draw' the candidate by personal example into the community of faith, to 'walk with *them*', and to 'help *them* to take their place within the life and worship of Christ's Church'.[8] The language of vows, so prominent in the *Book of Common Prayer* (1662), vanishes in the *Alternative Service Book* (1980), and only makes a return in *Common Worship* with the formula 'With the help of God, we will'. Nevertheless, each of our Anglican baptism liturgies demands *metanoia* (turning 'from' sin 'to' Christ) and a commitment to continue living in this way. Along with the physical symbolism of oil and water on the body of the

7 The traditional Anglican understanding of the relation between baptism and confirmation is discussed in more detail by Alex Hughes in the next chapter (Chapter 3).

8 When the candidates are 'able to answer for themselves', *Common Worship* envisages them being asked to commit to a more demanding series of vows, including to 'continue in the apostles' teaching and fellowship, in the breaking of bread, and in the prayers'; to 'persevere in resisting evil'; to 'proclaim by word and example the good news of God in Christ'; to 'seek and serve Christ in all people, loving your neighbour as yourself; to 'acknowledge Christ's authority over human society, by prayer for the world and its leaders, by defending the weak, and by seeking peace and justice' (p. 359).

candidate and the pronouncement of the trinitarian formula, baptismal vows thus contribute to the child's change in status, joining him or her to Christ in his death and resurrection, and making them a member of his Church/body/family. Baptism is thus a definitive moment of 'conversion', the first and decisive stage in a person's discipleship. As a minimum, the ASB envisages that this will include attendance at public worship and confirmation. In the latest baptism liturgies of the Church of England, what is expected is nothing less than full participation ('to take their place') and community ('walking together') in the body of Christ.[9]

The focus of the BCP and 1928 vows may seem more individualistic, until we remember that these vows are made 'by' the child 'through' others. The context is already a community. We thus find ourselves already located in a chain that stretches back through time. Someone has always already made these vows before us. The first person to answer on our behalf was Christ, who immediately after his baptism, rejected the devil and turned to his Father in perfect fulfilment of the commandments. It is Christ who first responded to God on our behalf: 'Here am I and the children whom God has given me' (Heb. 2.13).

We are therefore 'one body in Christ, and individually we are members one of another' (Rom. 12.5). It is this participation that makes possible the vicarious nature of baptismal vows. Many evangelicals object to infant baptism on the grounds that there is no possibility of conscious choice on the part of the child.[10] The classic response to this is that baptism symbolizes God's grace preceding any human action (including faith).

9 *Additional Baptism Texts in Accessible Language* (authorized for use from 1 September 2015) asks the whole congregation the following two questions: 'Will you support these children as they begin their journey of faith?' and 'Will you help them to live and grow within God's family?' See note 1 above.

10 The New Testament describes a decision for Christ as the combination of belief plus baptism: see Acts 16.31 and the longer ending of Mark's Gospel (Mark 16.16). It is for this reason that many baptism liturgies allow for a 'testimony' to be given by adult candidates, and why all baptisms include a confession of faith. Acts 10.44–48 and Acts 16.33 suggest that children may well have been baptized as part of the 'household' when a whole family came to faith. This would be consistent with the theme of inter-dependence and representative action on behalf of one another that is being developed in the present chapter.

Another answer suggested by my reading of baptismal liturgies would be that (a) people come to faith within communities, and (b) human beings can and regularly do enter into commitments vicariously, on behalf of other people. These realities are acknowledged through a variety of metaphors. In the BCP, godparents are described as 'sureties',[11] co-signatories to a debt in a manner that was once common and is now being revived through forms of community credit (such as loans made by the Grameen bank or credit unions). *Common Worship* prefers the metaphor of advocacy ('You speak for *them* today'). In both cases, the godparents assume responsibility for the baptized child. It may seem strange to speak of an infant making promises, as the BCP does, yet as Guido de Graaff has observed, it is through such practices that we reserve a place for the child as a future agent.[12] The goal is not individualistic independence for the child, but to further incorporate him or her into the life of *inter*-dependence that is the Church, a place where 'maturity does not equal autarky'.[13]

A Christian who is being drawn into the imitation of Christ will, like Christ, act vicariously on behalf of his or her neighbours, perhaps one day standing surety for them too, or making promises on their behalf.[14] At baptism, a person is joined to a network of mutually inter-dependent relationships that will continue to the end of their life, and beyond. Baptism therefore witnesses to a vision of humanity based on community and mutual responsibility, rather than on independence and individualism. It is much more than a matter of having the baby 'done', but rather of being remade with an explicitly eschatological end. To say that one wants one's children to 'decide for

11 The 1928 BCP retains the metaphor: 'this Child must also faithfully, for his part, promise by you that are his sureties (until he come of age to take it upon himself)' and asks the godparents to make commitments 'in the name of this Child'.

12 Writing in the *Church Times*, 19 February 2016.

13 De Graaff, Guido, 'Intercession as Political Ministry: Re-interpreting the priesthood of all believers' in *Modern Theology*, 32:4 (October 2016), p. 507.

14 In the typology devised by Sam Wells (2015) in *A Nazareth Manifesto: Being with God*, Chichester: Wiley Blackwell, this kind of advocacy corresponds to what Wells calls 'working for' or 'being for', while the sacramental incorporation into the body of Christ that takes place at baptism corresponds to Wells' 'being with'.

themselves' is therefore to miss the point. Their decisions will be made in the context of prior decisions made on their behalf. As we have seen, the 'Order of Confirmation' in the BCP sees the child's speech in just such terms, 'ratifying' and 'confirming' the decisions of others.

This brings us back to that phrase from the BCP, where 'you' (the candidates for confirmation) are called to renew the promises made 'in your name'. The practice of naming provides many parallels with the elements of calling-and-response that we have seen in God's relationship with us, and with the vicariousness of our human relationships. First, names are usually 'given', which means that they are prior to the individual's active choice, just as each of us is known and loved and called by God from before our birth. Secondly, just as baptism incorporates a person 'into Christ' and into the Church, so naming reserves a place for the child within the community. The purpose of a name is to allow one to be known (identified) and addressed (spoken of, spoken for, and spoken to). Naming acknowledges the place of a child within a web of wider relationships. This is particularly clear when the child is given the name of a relative, or is named after a saint.[15] Thirdly, a name is an invitation to participate in the game of language, naming others in one's turn. We see this process at work in the creation narratives. In Gen. 1, it is God who calls and names things, but in Gen. 2, God brings the animals to Adam 'to see what he would call them'. God delights in Adam's participation, as exemplified by his sharing of the power to name. When Adam names Eve in Gen. 2.23, it is not to demonstrate his authority over her (as has sometimes been suggested), but rather as a continuation of God's delight and an extension of God's invitation to participate in creation. In Gen. 4, it is Eve who names her children (see Gen. 4.1 and 4.25–26).

Names point to the 'scandal of particularity' that is at the heart of Christianity. God chooses to associate his name with the names of particular human beings, as 'the God of Abraham, the God of Isaac, and the God of Jacob' (Matt. 22.32). Baptiz-

15 The cryptic reference to baptism 'on behalf of the dead' in 1 Cor. 15.29 may describe such a practice.

ing new disciples 'in the name of the Father and of the Son and of the Holy Spirit' (Matt. 28.19) is a continuation of this impulse. There is truly something awesome here. It is about the bestowing a name on a particular human body, and in so doing associating it with the Name of the Holy Trinity, all while bringing that particular body into contact with water, with all its rich and terrifying elemental associations. Perhaps this is why baptism holds such resonance for trans people in particular.[16]

The givenness of most names suggests that other people often know us better than we know ourselves. This is not always the case, however. Sometimes other people give a name that seems wrong, as when Daniel is given the pagan name Belteshazzar (Dan. 1.7). But even when people name themselves, it is still possible that their new name may reveal the partial nature of their self-knowledge. Naomi calls herself 'Mara' (meaning 'bitter') in Ruth 1.20–21, but her neighbours come to disagree with this name (see Ruth 4.14–17). Only for God, who possesses perfect self-knowledge, is revealing his name identical with revealing himself (something that he refuses to do for Jacob, although he does give Jacob a new name to indicate the change that has come about in him, at Gen. 32.27–30). The names that God gives to Abram/Abraham and Jacob/Israel are promises. They prophesy and reveal a future state of affairs. The same is true of Jesus: 'they shall name him Emmanuel, which means, "God is with us"' (Matt. 1.23). It is Joseph, however, who gives him the name 'Jesus' (or Yeshua), which means 'God is our salvation'.

This orientation of names towards the future, as promises or expressions of hope, also means that they are provisional. Like the baptismal vows that were made on his or her behalf, a child's name remains provisional. For one thing, the child may choose new names for him- or herself, as in the traditional practice of taking a confirmation name or 'name in religion', but also as in the scenario of the trans person with whom we began. Names are contingent, social speech acts that affect our

16 I am indebted to Rachel Mann for this insight into the terrifying aspect of baptism.

horizontal relationships but have no effect on our baptismal identity in Christ. There is an eschatological element to names, as there is with baptismal vows. The whole truth about each person's identity is known only to God, and will only be revealed at the end of time. Ultimately, one's true identity is something that God will reveal.[17] This is the eschatological promise of Isaiah 62.2, 'you shall be called by a new name that the mouth of the LORD will give', and of Revelation 2.17, 'To everyone who conquers I will give ... a white stone, and on the white stone is written a new name that no one knows except the one who receives it.' All human language – of which names are a glorious example – remains provisional until the final revelation of all things in Christ.[18] It is thus true to say that identity is not something that we are born with, or that we create for ourselves, but a reality which we only discover gradually (or 'discern'). Name and identity are something towards which we are 'called': a vocation.

As with our names, so also our gender will look different at the eschaton. Jesus tells his disciples that 'in the resurrection they neither marry nor are given in marriage, but are like angels in heaven' (Matt. 22.30). This is not to deny the physicality of the resurrection of the body, but to sound a note of caution. We do not yet know what role gender will play eschatologically. Gender is at the heart of our experience of embodied personhood, but it is not the part that will ultimately define us. For the Christian, our identity 'in Christ' is our most basic and enduring identity. This point works as a summary of the argument we have been making so far. First, that human identity begins when God gratuitously calls things into being. Secondly,

---

17 Rowan Williams (1994) retells a parable that makes this point in his sermon 'Vocation (1)' in *Open to Judgement: Sermons and Addresses*, London: Darton, Longman and Todd, p. 176f.

18 We might attempt to draw some parallels with contemporary debates about gender. Is gender a 'given', for example? Or is it an invitation to participate in the co-creation of our identity (for example by our 'performances' of gender)? Adrian Thatcher (2016) offers a historical survey of the 'one gender' and 'two gender' theories in his book *Redeeming Gender*, Oxford: Oxford University Press. And for a slightly different contemporary discussion of these themes, see Douglas Farrow's blog article, 'The Right to Be Yourself? Gender Identity as the Baptism of Autonomy' at https://www.firstthings.com/web-exclusives/2017/03/the-right-to-be-yourself (accessed on 5 February 2022).

that Christ is the first to respond to God's call on our behalf. And thirdly, that we are baptized 'into Christ'. This is no initiation into a purely private individualism. Rather, baptism joins us to a pre-existing community within which our participation will come to have meaning as we become answerable for one another. The vows we make on behalf of one another, and the names we bestow are symbols of this. They create the language we are learning to speak, and in which we will eventually find our voices.[19]

It would seem, then, that there is a need for more teaching today about baptismal identity 'in Christ'. Identity is not simply a private matter, but is emphatically about joining a community of inter-dependent persons with mutual responsibilities to and for one another, including for vicarious action on one another's behalf. We need to hear from other people and from the call of God in our lives if we are ever to truly know ourselves. The seriousness and demand of this original baptismal 'calling' needs re-emphasis. This essay has also uncovered some confusion around the language of vows in our existing liturgies, and in the expression that they may give to the underlying theology just described. It will be important to regain clarity on the vows made at baptism as a response to God's prior call, an expression of *metanoia*, and an act of participation in the community that God is calling into being. This is especially important since baptismal vows are usually the first vows made in a person's life, and all subsequent vows (including those made at confirmation or marriage or ordination or profession) build on or intensify them. Finally, we have uncovered a theological need for listening one another into speech that is based on a commitment made at baptism. From

19 The idea of a 'voice' suggests a stable identity, but this is rather too smooth a description of the experience of growing up. There will of necessity be some discontinuities in people's experiences of their 'voice' (or name, or identity) over time, and this will be true for trans people just as it is for others. It should come as no surprise, then, that some trans Christians have spoken of their sex reassignment in the language of transformation or conversion: 'there is a huge part of me that is lost and can never be found' (Mann, Rachel, 2012, *Dazzling Darkness: Gender, Sexuality, Illness, and God*, Glasgow: Wild Goose Publications, p. 134), or saying 'My present is a changed life from my past' (Clare's story on transitioning was printed in the *Franciscan*, 28: 1 (January 2016), see p. 5).

this there arises a mutual responsibility to one another as the body of Christ. And most importantly for all of us, we have seen that our identity is only known by God and discovered gradually by us as we grow and learn through time. Insights into the truth about ourselves should thus always be greeted with awe and discerned with care.

3

The Role of Confirmation in the Vowed Life: A Reassessment

ALEX HUGHES

In this chapter Alex Hughes makes a bold challenge to the Church of England to refresh its theology of the vows of confirmation and rethink their significance for the life and renewal of the Church. The foundational significance of baptismal vows should not be seen as competing with, or rendering obsolete, the specific importance and challenge of confirmation. Rather, a loss of confidence in the importance of an intentional, considered, rite de passage *of commitment to Christ may be a self-defeating policy, and could partly explain why the allure of 'monastic' vows is, by way of compensation, now so attractive to many young people. For it is precisely an ascetic* demand *that calls forth the outworkings of the 'vowed life'.*

My brother used to work in the United Arab Emirates. I visited him once and we decided to drive from Dubai to Muscat in Oman. The road follows the coast along the Gulf. On the inland side there is almost nothing but desert. On the ocean side there is what seems like one long conurbation, extending all the way from the northern border of Oman to the capital. The largely unchanging surroundings made the journey quite dull, but I was struck by the layout of the inhabited side of the road, where the houses, schools, shops and places of work were punctuated at regular intervals by a mosque, into which the people flowed for the daily round of prayers. As I reflected on this I thought how the cities, towns and villages of England are also peppered with places of worship into which almost no one goes for the traditional offices of the Church (if they are observed at all).

Of course it is hard to compare the predominantly Ibadi Islamic culture of Oman with the religious habits of pluralist England. I mention the experience of my road trip only to highlight the fact that Christianity in England is not marked by intentional, corporate religious practice, apart from an hour on Sunday mornings. Though the Church has always enjoined its members to adopt daily devotions, they have largely remained the preserve of those Christians who live some sort of vowed 'Religious life' – monastics and clergy.[1] I know from my own experience as a parish priest that it often feels too much to expect people to come to church even once a week – something the Church of England seems to have accepted, from a statistical perspective at least, by counting 'regular attendance' as one Sunday per month. Yet I am haunted by some words of the journalist Andrew Brown: 'Only the churches that demand commitment from their members will get large numbers of committed members.'[2]

My experience of inner-city and rural ministry in particular has made me acutely aware that in many places the local church is kept alive by a few committed members, though sometimes that commitment seems to focus mainly on preserving historic buildings. As an archdeacon I observe that, as the number of churchgoers dwindles and the impact of theological tribalism becomes more pronounced in some areas, there is an undercurrent of competition between local churches, which encourages people to *consume* religion in a way that was unimaginable in years gone by. It is an ungodly irony that churches are increasingly seen as 'service providers', which has an inevitable impact on commitment: 'The church is in a buyer's market that makes any attempt to form a disciplined congre-

1 Anecdotal evidence suggests that the evangelical observance of a daily 'quiet time' has also declined considerably in recent decades.

2 'Tall, tattooed and forthright, can Nadia Bolz-Weber save evangelicalism?', in *The Guardian* (Saturday 6 September 2014), http://www.theguardian.com/commentisfree/2014/sep/06/tattooed-nadia-bolz-weber-save-evangelism-christianity (accessed 5 February 2022).

gational life very difficult.'[3] As Ian Cron's novel *Chasing Francis* suggests, too many church-people seem more like tourists than pilgrims.[4] There is a betrayal here of something essential to Christianity, for discipleship is not primarily about an individual or private spiritual journey, but about being transformed alongside others within the Body of Christ in order to model a new world order which makes the Gospel visible, so that the Church fulfils its vocation to be 'a sign, instrument and foretaste of the kingdom'.[5] My subject in this chapter, therefore, is about how we create a culture of *expectation* with respect to greater commitment; and I am led to wonder about the place of vows in this ambition by the fact that there is a growing body of Christians today who are looking for more committed or 'intentional' forms of Christianity than they find in their local church. I see 'new monasticism' as one way in which this desire is being met for some. New monasticism is the topic of another chapter in this volume, however,[6] and it is not my main concern here since I see it is a particular vocation rather than the kind of common commitment I want to think about. What seems lacking to me is a more general appreciation of the solemn calling to which believers are vowed simply by virtue of their Christian initiation. The roots of this in the baptismal vows are also discussed elsewhere in this book.[7] My focus is on confirmation, and my argument is that one way to reverse the increasing neglect of confirmation and to renew its importance in the life of the Church today, is to restore a focus on the confirmation vows. I realize that this may be something of an 'uphill struggle', so it is important to be frank about the current state of confirmation.

3 Hauerwas, Stanley, 2013, *Approaching the End*, Grand Rapids, MI: Eerdmans, p. x.

4 Cron, Ian Morgan, 2006, *Chasing Francis: A Pilgrim's Tale*, Grand Rapids, MI: Zondervan.

5 *The Meissen Agreement* (1991) I, available online at https://www.churchofengland.org/sites/default/files/2017-11/meissen_english.pdf (accessed 5 February 2022).

6 Chapter 8, below.

7 Chapter 2, above.

There is wide variety in terms of the practice and theology of confirmation in the Church of England, and it has become increasingly marginal in many churches.[8] The statistics are not encouraging: in the fourteen years from 2005 to 2019 the annual number of confirmations fell from 29,800 to 13,400 – a drop of 55%.[9] Anecdotal evidence suggests that some sections of the Church of England show little if any inclination to promote confirmation. There are (sometimes latent) theological drivers for this as traditional perspectives on Christian initiation change or lose purchase. One reason may be the promulgation of BACSI ('baptism as complete sacramental initiation'), which partly reflects the ecumenical spirit and desire to see as much of the fullness of Christianity as possible in traditions that do not practise confirmation. Although the theological work around BACSI has generally been done in high-level debate, it connects with grass-roots experience that 'conviction Anglicanism' is on the wane and many Church of England congregations are in fact multi-denominational by background. In such a setting, and in an effort to be as welcoming and inclusive of newcomers as possible, churches may minimize the importance of any need publicly to 'nail your colours to the mast'. In a slightly different vein, the widespread suspicion of institutions, in preference for 'authentic community', may militate against the use of confirmation if it is seen as a way of 'signing up' in the presence of the institutional boss (the bishop).[10]

8 I sometimes think Anglicans have become a little too complacent about the old saying, 'confirmation is a rite in search of a theology', treating it more as an excuse *not* to think about confirmation rather than a spur to think about it better. The Church of England's Liturgical Commission confessed that the *Common Worship* rite was drafted 'to take account of the fluid understanding of Confirmation in the Anglican Communion.' See: https://www.churchofengland.org/prayer-and-worship/worship-texts-and-resources/common-worship/christian-initiation/commentary (accessed 5 February 2022). The Faith and Order Commission's valedictory foray into the field also demonstrates the diversity of views and therefore did not leave this reader with any greater clarity (Avis, Paul (ed.), 2011, *The Journey of Christian Initiation: Theological and Pastoral Perspectives*, London: Church House Publications). This has surely served to make confirmation ever more marginal.

9 Statistics for Mission (2020): https://www.churchofengland.org/sites/default/files/2020-10/2019StatisticsForMission.pdf (accessed 5 February 2022).

10 I do not myself think that there is a necessary opposition between institutions and community – indeed, I tend to think that the point of institutions is to

Even where confirmation remains in regular use questions sometimes arise about its meaning and purpose. Its function as a rite of passage is perhaps mainly confined to older private schools, though these represent a high percentage of confirmations in some dioceses.[11] In some Church of England primary schools confirmation has become something like a 'graduation' for Year 6 pupils, which is not altogether unlike the scene among continental Protestants whose young people are confirmed in large numbers, but who seem to treat the ceremony as a kind of 'passing out parade' from which they never return. Back in England, I have heard of hopeful immigrants who have sought confirmation as a 'badge of Britishness'. And then there are the everyday tales of lament which clergy often tell (when they're not swapping funeral stories). My own contribution to this litany of woes comes from the time when, as a curate, I helped to prepare a group of young people for confirmation, all of whom had been baptized in infancy. One member of the group, 'Jane', decided not to be confirmed, because she wasn't sure of her faith. This was a disappointment, of course, but I also felt her responsible decision lent integrity to what we were doing. It was a bitter blow, however, to hear some years later that 'Peter', who *was* confirmed, became a Muslim soon after going to university.

Whatever may be said about the meaning and power of baptismal vows made by proxy, the fact that Jane (like so many others) later refused her baptismal identity is disturbing. And although Peter's somewhat dramatic 'apostasy' is much less common, a frank assessment must recognize a widespread abandonment or rejection of the kind of living faith and commitment envisaged by confirmation, which is also salutary. Notwithstanding the mixed practice and discouraging stories, however, I know from the five years I spent as a bishop's chaplain, and from my own parochial ministry, that there are

---

help foster and guard common life – but I recognize that there is a catalogue of institutional failures, within and outside the Church, which demands a degree of suspicion.

11 In fairness I should say that I have witnessed some exemplary work around confirmation in independent schools which belies the stereotype. Nevertheless, as a former public school-boy myself, I have first-hand experience of the 'herd mentality' too.

also many wonderful accounts of people for whom confirmation has been a decisive and deeply significant part of their faith-journey. So, without becoming too starry-eyed, my hope in this essay is to suggest that a re-emphasis on the vows might be a way to re-establish the place of confirmation in the life of the Church. There are difficulties, to be sure, but there are also possibilities. Next, though, we need some idea of what the confirmation vows are, and for this there is no escaping a liturgical history lesson.

To many people recently confirmed the idea that they made confirmation *vows* would come as a surprise, since the most recent liturgical texts are ambiguous in this respect. *Common Worship* makes no explicit mention of 'vows' in the context of baptism or confirmation, though its separate provision for the 'Corporate Renewal of Baptismal Vows' brings together three texts which are used in the initiation services under the three headings, 'Decision', 'Profession of Faith' and 'Commission'. As may be seen in the table below, the baptismal decision is not couched explicitly in the language of vows – that is, promises to do or be something – though the commission is. The 'Profession of Faith' is a dialogical form of the Apostles' Creed. It seems reasonable, therefore, to say that while the idea of 'vows' is implicit in the *Common Worship* initiation services (with confirmation vows being a renewal of baptismal vows) it is also obscured:

The Decision	**The Commission**
Do you reject the devil and all rebellion against God? **I reject them.** Do you renounce the deceit and corruption of evil? **I renounce them.** Do you repent of the sins that separate us from God and neighbour? **I repent of them.**	Will you continue in the apostles' teaching and fellowship, in the breaking of bread, and in the prayers? **With the help of God, I will.** Will you persevere in resisting evil, and, whenever you fall into sin, repent and return to the Lord? **With the help of God, I will.**

Do you turn to Christ as Saviour?
I turn to Christ.
Do you submit to Christ as Lord?
I submit to Christ.
Do you come to Christ, the way, the truth and the life?
I come to Christ.

Will you proclaim by word and example the good news of God in Christ?
With the help of God, I will.
Will you seek and serve Christ in all people, loving your neighbour as yourself?
With the help of God, I will.
Will you acknowledge Christ's authority over human society, by prayer for the world and its leaders, by defending the weak, and by seeking peace and justice?
With the help of God, I will.

Those who were confirmed using the *Alternative Service Book* [ASB] (1980) should be less surprised by the language of vows since the liturgy then had a clear heading, 'The Renewal of Baptismal Vows', after which followed three questions: 'Do you turn to Christ? **I turn to Christ.** Do you repent of your sins? **I repent of my sins.** Do you renounce evil? **I renounce evil'** – and a dialogical form of the Apostles' Creed. Again the questions and responses are not expressed strictly in the form of promises of intent, though the intentionality may reasonably be assumed.

The heading about the renewal of baptismal vows in the ASB is also found in the 'Alternative Order of Confirmation' contained in the 1928 proposed revision of the *Book of Common Prayer*, though in 1928 the texts that followed were different, and read more like a series of vows:

> Do ye here, in the presence of God, and of this congregation, renew the solemn promise and vow that was made in your name at your Baptism; ratifying and confessing the same in your own persons, and acknowledging yourselves bound to believe, and to do, all those things, which your Godfathers and Godmothers then undertook for you?

And everyone shall audibly answer, I do.
Or else the Bishop shall say,
Do ye here, in the presence of God, and of this congregation, renounce the devil and all his works, the pomps and vanity of this wicked world, and all the sinful lusts of the flesh, so that ye will not follow nor be led by them?
Answer. I do.
Do ye believe all the Articles of the Christian Faith as contained in the Apostles' Creed?
Answer. I do.
Will ye endeavour to keep God's holy will and commandments, and to walk in the same all the days of your life?
Answer. I will.

The proposed prayer book of 1928 retained the tradition stretching back to Cranmer's first prayer book (1549) of including a form of catechism prior to the confirmation service. These catechisms echo the pre-Reformation initiation rites of the *Sarum Manual*, which required the learning of certain texts as a normal qualification for confirmation. In the Sarum rite the texts were the Lord's Prayer, the Hail Mary, and the Apostles' Creed. In Cranmer's reformed prayer books they were the Apostles' Creed, the Lord's Prayer and the Ten Commandments. In the prayer books of 1549, 1559, 1662 and 1928, the catechism opens with a dialogue which clearly inspired the renewal of baptismal vows found in the 'Alternative Order' proposed in 1928:

Question. What is your Name?
Answer. *N*. or *M*.
Question. Who gave you this Name?
Answer. My Godfathers and Godmothers in my Baptism; wherein I was made a member of Christ, the child of God, and an inheritor of the kingdom of heaven.
Question. What did your Godfathers and Godmothers then for you?
Answer. They did promise and vow three things in my name. First, that I should renounce the devil and all his works, the pomps and vanity of this wicked world, and all the sinful

> lusts of the flesh. Secondly, that I should believe all the articles of the Christian faith. And thirdly, that I should keep God's holy will and commandments, and walk in the same all the days of my life.
> *Question*. Dost thou not think that thou art bound to believe, and to do, as they have promised for thee?
> *Answer*. Yes verily: and by God's help so I will. And I heartily thank our heavenly Father, that he hath called me to this state of salvation, through Jesus Christ our Saviour. And I pray unto God to give me his grace, that I may continue in the same unto my life's end.

From this historical survey we can see that the renewal of baptismal vows at confirmation has deep roots in the Church of England's liturgical tradition. Until the late-twentieth century there was a broadly agreed version of these vows: renunciation of the devil, the wicked world and the sinful flesh; belief in the articles of the Christian faith (enshrined in the Apostles' Creed); and commitment to keep the commandments of God (enumerated in the Decalogue). With the ASB came a revised three-fold formula, which *Common Worship* expanded into a six-fold version (later supplemented with a four-fold one).[12] In both the ASB and *Common Worship* the texts are less obviously vow-like.

While there is an evident lack of complete uniformity across the liturgical texts, and it is striking how forthright the *Book of Common Prayer* tradition is about vows compared with their obscurity in more recent forms, I think a generous-spirited critic might reasonably affirm a broad coherence, for they all require the confirmand to express repentance and renunciation of evil, faith in the person of Jesus, belief in the essential doctrines of Christianity and a commitment to living Christianly. But as yet we have no explanation as to why any of this has to

12 A supplementary text in 'accessible language' was authorized for use from September 2015, as follows: 'Do you turn away from sin? **I do.** Do you reject evil? **I do.** Do you turn to Christ as Saviour? **I do.** Do you trust in him as Lord? **I do.**' See: 2015, *Common Worship Christian Initiation: Additional Baptism Texts in Accessible Language*, London: Church House Publishing, p. 35.

be 'confirmed' by those who reach the 'years of discretion'.[13] Why may it not be taken for granted as a baptismal legacy?

Each of the prayer books prior to the ASB offers some rationale for the renewal of baptismal vows at confirmation, either in a series of prefatory rubrics (1549, 1559) or in a statement by the bishop at the beginning of the service (1662). The latter summarizes the content of the former, explaining that children who have reached the years of discretion:

> having learned what their Godfathers and Godmothers promised for them in Baptism ... may themselves, with their own mouth and consent, openly before the Church, ratify and confirm the same; and also promise, that by the grace of God they will evermore endeavour themselves faithfully to observe such things, as they, by their own confession, have assented unto.

The key terms here are 'consent', 'ratify', 'confirm', 'promise', 'confess' and 'assent', though it is not clear whether each of the six words is intended to carry a specific and different meaning (unlike, say, Cranmer's parenthesis in his eucharistic prayer – 'sacrifice, oblation, and satisfaction' – which is clearly an attempt to cover all the theological bases). In overlapping ways 'consent', 'ratify', 'confirm', 'confess' and 'assent' each indicate a mature appropriation of the baptismal vows formerly made by proxy, while 'promise' suggests the kind of forward-looking commitment associated with making a vow. In his essay on baptism[14] Joel Love has already helpfully drawn out the validity of vows made by proxy, which are based on the fundamentally communal formation of identity and belief. On this understanding the renewal of baptismal vows at confirmation has no retroactive significance: the baptismal liturgies simply assume that, with appropriate guidance and instruction, those who are baptized as infants will grow up to affirm Christian faith with their own mouth and from their own heart. The texts are

13 'Years of discretion' is commonly used in Church of England prayer books, and more widely and anciently, to describe the age at which confirmation becomes appropriate.

14 Chapter 2, above.

reverently (or judiciously) silent about what happens, or what it means, if children do *not* grow up to affirm their baptismal faith. It is time to think more about the 'years of discretion'.

Choosing an identity and a path for and on behalf of an infant is an unavoidable aspect of child-raising, though the choice may be made consciously and deliberately or unconsciously and haphazardly. As we shift attention from infant baptism to confirmation for those who have reached the years of discretion, however, the interplay of parental/communal and individual choice becomes complex.

On the eve of the Reformation the rites of Christian initiation in the West had evolved – some would say disintegrated[15] – into a sequence of four sacraments: baptism (at infancy), first confession, first Communion, and confirmation (either before or after first Communion depending on the availability of a bishop).[16] The latter three were administered at the age of seven, which was deemed to be the dawn of personal responsibility. It would be anachronistic to frame this coming of age in the typically modern terms of the autonomous human subject exercising freedom of choice, as may be seen in the maxim attributed to Ignatius Loyola (1491–1556), the founder of the Jesuits: 'Give me the boy for the first seven years and I will show you the man.' The formation of individuals within the life of the community was assumed, and conformity was expected. Presumably one reason for the traditional emphasis on learning certain devotional/liturgical texts by rote was not only to instruct but also to enculturate through participation.

Against this background it was reasonable to suppose that those who were baptized as infants would, with appropriate guidance and instruction, grow up to confirm their acceptance of the faith into which they were born. From the ninth century, when confirmation became established as a separate rite of initiation (in the Western Church), until at least the first half of

15 Such was the seminal thesis of J. G. Davies first aired in 'The Disintegration of the Christian Initiation Rite', *Theology* 50 (1947), pp. 407–12, and given classic exposition in Fisher, J. D. C., 1965, *Christian Initiation: Baptism in the Medieval West*, London: SPCK.

16 See e.g. Johnson, Maxwell E., 1999, *The Rites of Christian Initiation: Their Evolution and Interpretation*, Collegeville, MI: The Liturgical Press, ch. 6.

the twentieth century, there was good reason to expect that the baptismal initiation of infants would be fulfilled in confirmation and Communion (though to my knowledge the number of baptisms has always exceeded the number of confirmations, and there has been no golden age of church attendance). This pattern was, however, dependent on a Christian monoculture. The wane of Christendom means that people are not formed within a single worldview and have to exercise at least some degree of personal judgement about how they understand themselves and the world: being Christian is increasingly an active choice rather than a cultural activity. But it is a matter of debate how free this choice is, since we are inescapably historical beings, so to an extent we are both created and constrained by social, cultural and historical forces of which we may have limited awareness, let alone control. (This is, of course, the tactical assumption of the advertising industry as it forms our desires in order to help us 'freely' make commercially favourable choices.) The problem for the Church, though, in its desire to inculcate sincere commitment in its members, is that, as Walter Brueggemann stresses, Christians find themselves in a new kind of exile, and highly susceptible to Babylonian definitions and modes of reality. It would be foolish to deny that there are degrees of capitulation, however unconscious, while in more reactionary circles religious hierarchs (often in bland, culturally inconspicuous clothing) patrol the cultural boundaries strenuously, resorting to 'coercive authoritarianism and moralistic maintenance of Christian identity'.[17] The challenge for those who value the spirit of freedom in the gospel is how to support and sustain Christian identity through voluntary patterns of belief and practice – voluntary in the sense of freely chosen, but of a different character to ephemeral modern 'lifestyle' choices. As public, and to an extent corporate, choices and statements of personal intent, the confirmation vows might contribute more to this, if only there was more emphasis on the scope and scale of the demand.

---

17 Brueggemann, W., 1997, *Cadences of Home*, Louisville, KY: Westminster John Knox Press, p. 41.

At this point it is important to take stock of the complex dialectic in a theological understanding of *choice*. As I have already pointed out, the modern world still tends to think of choice in Enlightenment terms as the exercise of unfettered freedom of thought and will by autonomous human subjects. There is value in this conception of human being, despite its deconstruction as a myth, but it clashes (quite deliberately) with a traditional religious view, rooted in the biblical themes of creation and election, which invests God with a primary and prevenient choice that in some way conditions all of our choices. I do not pretend to have worked out this dynamic completely or systematically in my own mind, but I have some direct experience of it in my inner life, by which I mean that I can't really disentangle a sense of choosing from being chosen.[18] The general point, though, is that a properly Christian account of confirmation must start with some idea of what God is up to (so to speak).

If there is a desire to imbue confirmation with greater power and significance, at least at an imaginative level, then this must be through the articulation of a divine *call* – a summons to a devout and holy life which the believer hears with due trepidation, certainly, but perhaps also with conviction-generating excitement. This is, in fact, deep-rooted in the confirmation liturgy as the bishop anoints each candidate before the laying on of hands, saying, 'God has called you by name and made you his own' (cf. Isa. 43.1). In this light the vows may be seen as a commitment to (try to) be what we already are. The parenthesis in the last sentence is important as we seek to appreciate the dynamic of the vows, which parallels the mystery of divine and human choice. What I mean is that at confirmation we hear the proclamation of God's indicative, 'You are mine,' but we can't quite respond straightforwardly in the indicative, 'Yes I am,' because we know that in our fallen human freedom we often choose to belong to ourselves and stay captive to our idols. Instead, we *vow* our intent to let our lives be conditioned

18 There are seldom any feelings of vainglory associated with a sense of being chosen, partly because it is so obviously unmerited, and also because the witness of the Bible and tradition suggest that being chosen by God often means being marked out for suffering.

by what in God's good time (eschatologically) we will be. Or, to put it the other way round, the confirmation vows work proleptically as they lay hold of the promised future (which is God's eternal now, God's indicative) in order to give shape to the historical present.

This interpretation connects with a once-common account of the effect of confirmation, which was to *strengthen* the believer. Historically, this strengthening was seen to be important in connection with reaching the years of discretion, the dawn of personal responsibility, which broadly coincided with the conscious experience of temptation (especially of a sexual nature). This idea of strengthening may still be important; but here I want to emphasize the power of the *vows* as they give voice to a wish or desire for the fulfilment now of a glimpsed future reality.[19] Secular analogues of this potency might be the skill of 'acting as if' in Cognitive Behavioural Therapy or the practice of 'visualization' in life coaching. I see no reason to draw a categorical distinction between these and 'spiritual' forms of transformation, since I assume that however the Holy Spirit works in us it must be through our common humanity, with all its evolved biological, emotional and psychological processes; however, I would add that the confirmation vows give strength because they tap into the power of divine reality.

In the first act of *King Lear*, as his faculties begin to unravel the king asks, 'Who is it that can tell me who I am?' Although it is risky these days to make statements about universal human nature, I strongly suspect that the enduring power of Shakespeare's drama has something to do with the fact that it very often coincides with people's experience of their own reality, so I am ready to suppose that Lear's identity crisis is commonplace. In late- or post-modernity this crisis has become even sharper as there is now considerable resistance to the idea that people have a fixed identity. Personal identity is commonly seen as something *performed* rather than something *given*. It is hard to say where the contemporary popular emphasis on

19 In this way we meet God's indicative with a subjunctive (hopeful) or optative (desiring) mood. On this point see Ford, David F., 2007, *Christian Wisdom: Desiring God and Learning in Love*, Cambridge: Cambridge University Press, 2007, pp. 45–51.

self-actualization lies between these two poles, since it seeks the full expression and activation of every (given?) capacity and potential, but in attitude it stands against the idea that anyone should feel restricted or constrained in terms of what they might do or be, and it therefore eschews the kind of lasting commitment expressed in a religious vow. In fairness, this is probably a caricature, since most people do seem to live in a way that suggests a link between integrity and identity; and probably most people would accept that every positive choice necessarily entails the rejection of other possibilities. But even so, it still feels countercultural to commend the idea that personal identity can *only be fully realized through a binding, life-long vow*.

If Lear's question does indeed form in everyone's heart at some time, in one way or another, the confirmed Christian can bear witness to his or her personal experience that at confirmation God meets our 'Who am I?' with 'I have called you by name' – that is to say, I have given you an identity. This given identity is not understood as a restriction, however, and, as I have described above, it is waiting to be performed. The common vows have to be lived out by individual people, each with their own unique strengths and gifts (and frailties and disabilities), and there are many paths to choose between at every step on the journey of life. The identity to which we bind ourselves at confirmation is something much deeper than any of this, however. It is the truly radical sense of identity as a creature before the Creator; for God finishes the sentence, 'I have called you by name ...' with '... you are mine'. Through confirmation, therefore, we vow to let our urgent, anxious, dependent query, 'Who am I?' deepen into the profoundly transformative, because worshipful, 'Whose am I?' In this sense, confirmation is even more about belonging than it is about believing. The Christian witness that arises from this experience is to a liberation, for the fundamental givenness of our identity frees us from any fear that it could be put in question by the quality of our performance. The Christian idea of freedom is not like that of the Enlightenment, proclaiming the autonomy – and therefore the *responsibility* – of the individual subject: it is the freedom that comes from discovering the joy of being a child of God –

God's choice, not ours. I see this as a crucial antidote to the potentially devastating effect on those who experience failure – and who doesn't? – yet were indoctrinated by Lin Marsh's humanist popular song 'Believe', in which primary school children are told they can be and do anything they want just so long as they believe in themselves. What an appalling weight of responsibility! One advantage of the interpretation of the confirmation vows I have outlined above is that it can embrace the universal experience of failure without undermining the sincerity of intention. While it is right that we should approach the confirmation vows with the 'fear of the Lord', since they are truly momentous, there is also no reason to put them off until death is nigh and there is no time for hypocrisy. To do so would be to miss their point, which is that they commit us to living in God's time – the place where we truly belong, whether we live up to it or not. Seldom has this been expressed more powerfully than in Dietrich Bonhoeffer's prison poem, 'Who am I?', which makes no attempt to gloss over the self-doubt and painful contradictions entailed in trying to live up to his Christian profession, but ends with a chastened confidence: 'Who am I? They mock me, these lonely questions of mine. / Whoever I am, Thou knowest, O God, I am thine!'[20]

It might be thought foolish to suggest that a renewed emphasis on confirmation vows could be a panacea for the contemporary Church's enfeeblement and decline. However, I do think that a tendency to downplay this aspect of Christian commitment, as illustrated in the liturgical revisions that have obscured it, is a profound mistake. I accept it is not obvious how this would have made any difference to my potential confirmand 'Jane' all those years ago, since she was clearly and responsibly not ready to make a further Christian commitment. But might it have helped to keep 'Peter' in the fold? Of course I can't answer that question. Maybe if the Church had been more confident about calling upon confirmands to make solemn vows I might have done more and better to impress upon Peter the significance, demand and power of what he was undertaking,

20 Bonhoeffer, Dietrich, 2010, *Works, Volume 8: Letters and Papers from Prison*, translated by Nancy Lukens et al. and edited by Eberhard Bethge et al., Minneapolis: Fortress Press, p. 459

and he might have found the additional energy and inspiration that commitment often brings. Maybe. If I were in a position now to bring people to confirmation, I certainly would make much more of the vows, and perhaps lead from them into a (partly post-confirmation) exploration of a Rule of Life to help plot the steps of intentional living and growing into the fullness of Christian identity. An emphasis on living out the vows helps with the transition from celebration of confirmation as a one-off sacramental act into an ongoing pattern of committed believing.

The idea of binding, life-long promises may be countercultural today, but I believe that it is a core part of what it means to be 'in' though not 'of' the world. Christians are 'resident aliens' trying to inhabit God's time.[21] The habitat of the Kingdom requires the intentional cultivation of a new *habitus*, of which the confirmation vows are a mature expression. The renewal of baptismal commitment by those who have reached the age of maturity proclaims something vital about Christian freedom within God's providence. To make these vows is to trust that I will know myself truly as I try to live, under the aegis of the Spirit, into the promised truth about myself.

21 Hauerwas, Stanley and Willimon, William H., 1989, *Resident Aliens: Life in the Christian Colony*, Nashville: Abingdon Press.

4

Marriage: Vowing to Take Time

MATTHEW BULLIMORE

In this chapter Matthew Bullimore begins with a poignant vignette from his own parish life to illustrate the current anxieties and confusions in the Church of England about the nature of marriage and the importance of vows to it. As in Joel Love's chapter on baptism and (gender) identity, so here also a contemporary theological conundrum about marriage leads into a deeper reconsideration of the special meaning of marriage vows, their implicit rootedness in baptismal vows, and their distinctiveness as a restriction of options which is at the same time an openness to the freedom of the future – a commitment by the partners to 'take time' with each other for the sake of the Kingdom, the Church and the wider society.

So far in this book we have reconsidered the foundational significance of baptismal vows in the Christian life, and then underscored afresh how significant confirmation vows are as an entry into conscious re-commitment to those vows at a liminal moment of challenge and choice.

Now we come to marriage, another momentous point of personal decision in which vows are central. Everyone knows that. But marriage vows differ from the other vows in this book. In Christian marriage, vows are made to another person in the presence of God rather than to God in the presence of other people. The Church of England also recognizes marriages that are contracted as part of *civil* ceremonies with their own forms of vows. This makes for a complex scenario which may be confusing to those on the edges of church life.

I was surprised nonetheless to receive the following unsolicited text message in the course of normal parish business: 'Do you do *civil weddings* at your church?' That's all it said. I hit the roof. I know that people are married in these churches because they are pretty and they fulfil the fairy-tale dream. I flinch when couples ask to 'book' the church as if were a venue rather than asking me to organize a service. Nevertheless, whatever their expectations, I prepare each couple for the *Christian* service of marriage in which they will participate. We tease out the reasons why they want to be married, and in public, and in a community setting, and what has brought them to want to make vows to one another – after all, no-one should come just for the romantic theatre of it. All of that is put in the context of God's love for the couple and his world. So the idea that I would allow a civil registrar to take a wedding in church – even if I legally could – was unthinkable.

Thankfully, reason prevailed over my galloping rage. Who on earth would even *want* a civil wedding in a church? But then the light bulb lit up.

I rang the couple. 'Keeley' answered. She and her partner would like to get married in church but they were not sure if that sort of thing is allowed. I asked her what her partner was called. 'Abi.' Ah. 'Come round and have a chat,' I said.

This all happened not long after the bishops issued their 'pastoral letter' about equal marriage (15 February 2014).[1] I

1 As I heard one bishop say, 'An odd title really given that it was neither pastoral nor a letter.' It can be read at: https://www.churchofengland.org/news-and-media/news-and-statements/house-bishops-pastoral-guidance-same-sex-marriage (accessed 5 February 2022). This statement followed not long after the Church of England's Pilling Report (Pilling, Joseph (chair), 2013, *Report of the House of Bishops Working Group on Sexuality*, London: Church House Publishing) which had recommended that there may be circumstances when a priest should be free to mark the formation of a permanent same-sex relationship. Nonetheless, the report's recommendations were not unanimous among the working group and the report included a dissenting statement. The recommendations led to a process of 'Shared Conversations' across the Church from 2014–16, which in turn resulted in the 2017 report 'Marriage and Same Sex Relationships after the Shared Conversations'. The motion to 'take note' of what was seen by some as a disappointingly conservative report fell in the General

had a wonderful chat with Keeley and Abi. They told me all about why they wanted to get married in a church as part of a religious ceremony with vows.

I had to tell them I simply could not legally marry them but I could certainly find some way to pray with them. They were delighted that something could be done, although they were anxious that it would put *me* in an awkward position. We took it from there.

Now that there is a civil form of marriage that the Church of England does *not* recognize (that is, marriage between same-sex couples), the Church is presented with an imperative once again to think through the nature of vowed relationships between couples; and especially so because, whatever their reasons, people are still continually coming to churches and seeking to make their vows there.

In welcoming people into church to be prepared for marriage the Church has the opportunity to proclaim why making marriage vows before God grants marriage a new social meaning which is a benefit to the whole community. Marriage is a communicative action, one that in being gracefully transformative of the couple is also transformative of the wider society.

Marriage is, of course, a notoriously complicated institution to write about. I will not be able to discuss the many and varied understandings of marriage throughout history (before and during the Christian era) or across traditions, cultures and religions, nor pinpoint exactly what it is which is the essential nature of marriage (e.g., is it unitive, procreative, sacramental, romantic, or necessarily heterosexual?).[2]

In what follows I look more closely at the vows as they are found within the liturgy of the Church and focus on how marriage as a vowed life asks us to make use of the *time* that God gives us – a time in which he is preparing us all for life with him by teaching us how to love and be loved. Marriage

---

Synod after the House of Clergy failed to win a majority of votes. This in turn led to the project Living in Love and Faith which invites further conversation, study and prayer.

2 Some of these issues are discussed briefly in an earlier Littlemore Group book: see Laing, Catriona, 2017, 'Office: Marriage', in Martin, Jessica and Coakley, Sarah (eds), *For God's Sake: Re-Imagining Priesthood and Prayer in a Changing Church*, Norwich: Canterbury Press, pp. 91–106.

vows can teach us what time it is that we are living in – a time oriented towards the coming of the Kingdom in all its fullness.

It is important to emphasize at the outset that for the New Testament *all* redeemed social relationships are taken up within the overarching nuptial analogy of Christ's relationship with his multifaceted bride, the Church. It is in that context that I will also be suggesting that we might be able to recognize as a social good other loving vowed relationships – whether or not they are called 'marriages' – because of the way that they – precisely *as vowed* – teach us how to love and be loved in this time in which God is preparing us for union with him.

Giving Consent to Go to School

The preface to the *Common Worship* marriage service tells us how a couple will enter marriage as a *way of life*. They will give consent, make solemn vows, give and receive a ring. The marriage is also declared by the joining of hands. The vows are framed by various declared intentions and are set within a series of ritual actions that dramatize the life of mutual recognition and regard over time.

The declaration of consent, in which the will of each person to marry is established, first notes that the couple *take* one another. It is a dynamic movement: both an active movement to *reach out* for another to form a new kinship group, and a *reception* of the other from the primary kinship networks in which they are already situated. In taking the other, they promise to love, comfort, honour and protect him/her. Each partner will seek the welfare of the other as their own welfare (cp. Eph. 5.21–33).

The declaration ends with the promise of fidelity while both partners live. Faithfulness here includes the exclusivity of sexual relations, but it is less understood today as a form of ownership so much as a recognition of the responsibility to seek the good and fulfilment of this other one *in particular*.

The promise of mutual faithfulness is an acceptance that it takes time to attend truly to another and in so doing to learn to love him or her well and to accept that we ourselves are loved.

Eugene Rogers argues that the vows commit the couple into 'a community from which one cannot easily escape', and one in which they are exposed and vulnerable before the other. They 'undertake the long and difficult commitment over time and place to find themselves in the perceptions of another.'[3] He follows Rowan Williams in arguing that marriage is, in this sense, a school that prepares us to see that we are loved by God.[4] And just as God's love is not finally dyadic, but the love of Father and Son overflows through the grace of the Holy Spirit, so the faithful exclusivity of the married couple allows them, in learning how to love *this one* well, to learn how better to love others. Love spills out. This begins to undermine the idea that marriage is just something romantic or only dyadic but shows it to be expansive. As one specific mode of life within the body of Christ, founded in baptism, it is one of the ways in which the Church as a whole learns how to love. So the prayers in the *Common Worship* marriage service point to the way in which a marriage is to foster hospitality, care and nurture – of family and also of strangers.

Love spills out but love is also received back again. The couple are held with care by the community that surrounds them. Just as Christ's gift of himself to the Father in loving service and obedient response is witnessed by the Spirit, so the couple's exchange of self-giving love is also witnessed. The human witnesses pledge to support and uphold the couple who are now marking out a new way of life in the midst of the community.

Supremely, it is God who is present as the witness of this public act. In ancient forms of covenant making, the divine witness was the guarantor. For Israel, even when God is a covenant partner, it is still God's promise of faithfulness that ratifies and guarantees the covenant. For Christians, it is Christ's faithfulness that is finally salvific (Rom. 3.21–26; 1 Cor. 1.9; 1 Thess.

3 Rogers, Jr, Eugene F., 2006, 'Trinity, Marriage, and Homosexuality', in Mark D. Jordan (ed.), *Authorizing Marriage? Canon, Tradition, Critique in the Blessings of Same-Sex Unions*, Princeton: Princeton University Press, pp. 162–3.

4 See Williams, Rowan, 2002, 'The Body's Grace', in Rogers, Jr, Eugene F., (ed.), *Theology and Sexuality: Classic and Contemporary Readings*, Oxford: Blackwell, pp. 309–21.

5.24; Heb. 2.17). So, in marriage, the couple's action is put in the context of Christ's work – and that is the direction of the marriage analogy used in Eph. 5. God's relationship to us is not simply reminiscent of our covenanted loving relationships. Human marriage is a sign of the primary nuptial relationship of Christ to his Church; marriage is given for this purpose – to bear witness to God's faithful love of us.

Vowing ...

At a marriage rehearsal – however much horseplay there may be – the practising of the vows always marks a change in atmosphere. There may be nervous giggling or even crying but there is a palpable sense that the vows to be made are serious and life-changing. People understand that this is a dramatic moment.

As the couple come to the marriage vows they turn to one another. The 'taking' mentioned in the declaration of consent is now performed by the giving away of the bride. The patriarchal overtones remain – it is the bride who is 'given away' – but the bridegroom also puts his hand into the bride's hand for his vows.[5] It is a dual act, albeit asymmetrical, in which the couple dramatize the fact that each is a gift to the other and also a gift from one kinship group to another. They form a new third (affinal) kinship association which itself becomes a gift to be received back by the donors and changes their relationships with one another (when couples ask if they have to have 'sides' in the service I suggest that it doesn't really matter since we will all be family by the end).

The intimacy of the moment when the vows are made mirrors the intimacy that is shared within the marriage. Here the partners name one another as this particular one, looking at them as the primary focus of life-long regard. Each is physically held by the other, for this union is a bodily one – and one that for all its symbolic and theological reference cannot be spiritualized

5 Interestingly, Jesus quotes Genesis (Mark 10.6–9; see Gen. 2.24) which stresses that it is the *man* who leaves his father and mother to be joined to his wife.

away. It is only in bodily enactment that the symbolic associations will be meaningful – just as the union of divinity and humanity in Christ is a bodily and personal matter.[6]

The vows reflect the changes and chances of life that may affect the married couple in their bodily life together. They concern external circumstances over time in terms of economic wellbeing, health and chance. So the couple take one another 'from this day forward for better and for worse, for richer, for poorer, in sickness and in health' to be loved and cherished until 'death us do part'. Note how the vows use comparative words – better, worse, richer, poorer. Unlike so many self-authored vows, which tend to profess things in the absolute ('I will always be there', 'I will never let you down', 'you will always be my honey-bunny-woo-woo'), the marriage vows recognize that the path might be steep and love will have to be hardy. The vows are realistic about this, foregrounding the stresses and strains that will assail the couple and the joys that will accompany easier times.

Marriage is to be life-long and truly a way of life for them both from this moment forward. Yet this is to acknowledge that marriage is a continuing set of encounters with one another and that *we* change over time just as circumstances will change. The people we are when we marry will not be the people we are in years to come by dint of shared experience and the nature of human living. A choice is being made in which we are bound together to live out the consequences of that choice.

... to Take Our Time

This extension over time is key to marriage as a vowed way of life, and implicitly of course it builds upon what vows mean in the foundational context of baptism. These marriage vows are not vows that entail only a change in state or the establishment of a new form of relationship. They must endure. The vow is

6 See Loughlin, Gerard, 2007, 'Introduction: The End of Sex', in Loughlin, Gerard (ed.), *Queer Theology: Rethinking the Western Body*, Oxford: Blackwell, p. 6.

a promise, and a promise comes with two parts that top and tail an extension over time. First of all there is the pledge, and eventually there is the fulfilment (note that a threat has the same structure). The pledge is made, but the promise is only ever seen as truthful – as having been kept – when it is fulfilled.[7]

In *Common Worship*, the vows end with, 'in the presence of God I make this vow.' This is the first time in Anglican liturgy that make reference to the vows being made in God's presence. Echoing the reminder in the 'Preface' that Jesus was present at the wedding in Cana, the vows are set within the frame of his faithfulness to us. These vows are promises but the form of words here lacks something of that sense of promissory duration (although, of course, we have just heard that the vows last until death parts the couple). The 1980 *Alternative Service Book* [ASB] had each partner end the vows with: 'and this is my solemn vow'. This was a rather bland and formal modernization of 1966's *Series One*[8] liturgy where both partners ended the vows with 'and thereto I give thee my troth' (which was itself the ending to the bride's vows in the 1662 *Book of Common Prayer* [BCP]). What is noteworthy about the form of words in *Series One*, and which is lost in the ASB and *Common Worship*, is that we can see here that something is being *given*. Something is being *ventured* in being given away.[9]

But perhaps the best formulation for signalling the importance of *duration* is the (culturally recognizable) ending to the bridegroom's vows in the BCP: 'and thereto I *plight* thee my troth.'[10]

---

7 For an extended discussion of this theme, see Walter, Gregory, 2013, *Being Promised: Theology, Gift, and Practice*, Grand Rapids, MI: Eerdmans.

8 *Series One* was the name given to the now authorized version of the changes to the 1662 *Book of Common Prayer* which were initially proposed unsuccessfully in 1928.

9 *Series One* actually equalizes the vows for the first time so that both partners could make exactly the same vow. The proposed 1928 revisions to the BCP had moved towards equality by removing the clause in which only the bride vows to 'love, cherish and obey'. Nevertheless 'and obey' crept back in as an *option* in *Series One*, and remained in the ASB and *Common Worship*. Note too that it was in the ASB that rings were first *exchanged* as a sign of mutuality.

10 I have been unable to discover the significance of the discrepancy in the BCP vows although I suspect it has something to do with the respective legal statuses of men and women.

The noun 'plight' is not fortuitous, referring as it does to a sad, difficult or unpleasant condition. Yet the verb form can mean something like 'to bind one by a pledge.' Indeed, it is a form of giving in pledge as in 'I give you my word.' It offers as a guarantee something that is noble – as when we say 'on my word', or 'on my honour'. Something is given which is thus endangered or put at risk should the pledge not be fulfilled. It is proffered and ventured and would lead to the ruination of the one who pledges if it is not honoured. Here what is 'plighted' is 'troth' or my truth, good faith, faithfulness, honesty and loyalty. It is a promise to be true – to remain true always – to this one only in all circumstances. The fulfilment of that pledge can only finally be seen at the end of the marriage, the point of death. Like the good life, our troth can only be finally judged backwards.

As with the covenants God makes with his people Israel, there is a promise that extends between a pledge and its fulfilment. The vows are made in the presence of God, the primary guarantor and witness, and so partake of a duration that is of God. It is God's time that is given to us as a gift in which we learn to love, trust and orient ourselves in hope towards the fulfilment of a promise. In that time we learn to enjoy the fruits of that pledge through our trusting attention to the other over time. Marriage vows give us the time we need to undertake our labour of love, to nurture one another in friendship and 'to grow together in love and trust'. It is the time in which we learn through the discipline of loving one another what it is to be loved by God – for 'God is love and those who live in love live in God and God lives in them' (1 John 4.16). In that sense it is a time of sanctification, because it prepares us for life with God as we learn to love this person in particular, and, in so doing, others too.

Christian Time

The vows made as part of a Christian marriage participate in and symbolize time as Christians understand and experience it. If the marriage vows reveal that marriage is about the duration of a promise, then they resonate with the time in which we live – the time between Christ's coming and his coming again – what has been called the 'time between the times' or the time that remains before time comes to an end. In 1 Corinthians, Paul talks about being the one 'on whom the ends of the ages have come' (10.11), for the old age is passing away and the new age is breaking in (1 Cor. 7.31; Gal. 6.14–15).

When the New Testament speaks about marriage, it is as something that needs to be practised differently because Jesus has come and all has been made new. Marriage language becomes inseparable from language about the Church ('This is a great mystery, and I am applying it to Christ and the Church' (Eph. 5.32)). It has become an eschatological language that describes the relationship between Christ and his people both now (Matt. 9.15; John 3.29) and in the age to come (Rev. 19.7–8). Marriage as vowed, as a relationship in time set between promise and fulfilment, reflects and shares in the time in which Christians live.

For Paul, the old structures of the world and the powers that sustained it have been deactivated and disempowered by Christ. Although many things continue as they did before, they do so in a new light. We may remain in the condition to which we were originally called (1 Cor. 7.17–20), but we now 'make use' of those conditions in the light of all things being renewed in Christ (1 Cor. 7.21, 24; 2 Cor. 5.17). Marriage, as something originally created as a gift (Mark 10.6–9), is now to be seen in this new situation:

> I mean, brothers and sisters, the appointed time has grown short; from now on, let even those who have wives be as though they had none, and those who mourn as though they were not mourning, and those who rejoice as though they were not rejoicing, and those who buy as though they had no possessions, and those who deal with the world as though they had no dealings with it. For the present form of the world is passing away. (1 Cor. 7.29–31)

Paul has plenty to say about marriage and initially seems to see it as a concession to those with little self-control and as a second-best to a life of celibacy (1 Cor. 7.8–9). But he also speaks of it positively as a life that sanctifies even an unbelieving partner (1 Cor. 7.12–16). Paul does not countenance divorce as the right course of action for aligning ourselves with this new age, for we are to remain in the conditions in which we were called. Instead, we *make use* of those conditions. We live in them *as not* in them – we live in them in a way no longer consonant with the old age but live in them in this 'messianic' age in anticipation of the age to come. It is as if to say we have spouses, yes, but do not have them as we used to.

So it is that the marriage vows with their witness to this time of promise begin to 'trouble' existing understandings of marriage in this age. They become signs of God's promises to his people in this new time (as they were signs of promise throughout the first covenants – e.g., Hos. 2.16–23 and Isa. 62). Even as something temporal and provisional unto death – as something irreducibly partial and *secular* – they become signs of the promise of new life and eternal union of Christ with his people in the wedding feast to come (Rev. 21.2, 9). Marriage receives an eschatological and universal horizon. Paul might see marriage as a concession against inflamed passion, but on the other hand marriage is also clearly the best symbol the New Testament writers can find to describe the impassioned love of God for his people to whom he has united himself in Jesus.

The apocalyptic tone of Paul's discussion of marriage does not call for the dissolution of identities, but seeks to see what they now are *in Christ*. Understanding them in the context of this new age in which we await the fulfilment of what Christ pledged in his incarnate and risen life with us actually opens up our identities and our relationships and transfigures them. The eschatological social life that they prefigure must transform how we now perform them. Marriage has become a particular mode – one that is particularly symbolically loaded – of participating alongside others in the common life of the Church, the bride who is being united to Christ. All of those relationships that make up the life of the bride are drawn, through union with Christ, into the joy of the life of shared love that is the Trinity.

Thus marriage as a *vowed* life is of this age but it is also used to symbolize the life to come. It is provisional ('till death us do part') and partial ('forsaking all others'), but it is a sign to be used by the whole people to understand their relationship to God. Marriage *surpasses* itself. It is no longer something that could only be about property rights, cultural transmission, the perpetuation of a blood-line, inheritance or posterity. It has now become symbolic of a new form of life in Christ, even as it already shares in it now.

Marriage and Children

How might we understand how marriage is performed anew in the time between the times? Marriages have always been associated with having children, and so let us take that as an example. As about children, marriage is also about death. As St John Chrysostom said: 'Where there is death there is marriage'.[11] In other words, marriages produce children because people die. This is true, but the New Testament makes us think differently about even that.

When Jesus is questioned by the Sadducees about the resurrection, his response offers a critique of their understanding of marriage (Luke 20.27–40). They point to the law that if her husband dies a woman must marry her husband's brother. By such a 'taking' of the woman by the brother, the deceased husband's line, name and posterity is preserved. The Sadducees question the resurrection on the grounds that it would be absurd to think that a woman could have several husbands in the life to come. Jesus argues that those 'of this age' – oriented to the principles and values of this world – give and are given in marriage. Those who are of the age to come, oriented to life with God, do not marry as if it were part of the death-oriented economy that the Sadducees perpetuate. Those who live with faith in the resurrection live lives that are without the need to buy insurance against death through posterity. Jesus seems to relativize the need for children by arguing that those who live life oriented towards the life to come are themselves 'children of

11 John Chrysostom, *On Virginity*, 14.6, quoted in Song, Robert, 2014, *Covenant and Calling: Towards a Theology of Same-Sex Relationships*, London: SCM Press, p. 15.

God'. No longer is their worth determined by honour, prestige and wealth but by how far they live as children of God ('Love your enemies, do good, and lend expecting nothing in return ... and you will be children of the Most High' (Luke 6.35)).

All of our relationships are reoriented by putting them in an eschatological context – including marriage. No longer need women be objectified for the sake of the demands of laws concerning the continuation of a heritage. Instead, all people find their worth by being oriented to the life and values of the world to come. The present form of marriage is rendered inoperative and otiose. Marriage will be renewed when it shares in the renewed social life of the Kingdom. It is no longer something instrumental to the perceived social goods of this age but is a vowed covenant that bears witness to God's promise to fully establish his Kingdom – a new social existence in Christ. In other words, marriage as taking the time of a promise, as reflecting Christian time, can begin to reveal to us that what guarantees our future is not family but the Church, the harbinger of the Kingdom to come.[12]

As both Robert Song and Stanley Hauerwas stress, this is not to deny that procreation has any theological import. It is an image of God's creative fruitfulness and also witnesses to our hope in God's continuing involvement in the time that remains. God has not abandoned his world and the building of his Kingdom he does in time. That is, the Church's vocation to witness to his redeeming love to the nations takes time. Children are not vehicles for the transmission of a name or a line but the gift to the Church today that it might also continue to witness tomorrow.

Thus marriage and procreation must be redrawn when they are seen as sharing in the priorities and form of life of the age to come. Marriage becomes disruptive of any this-worldly focus. It is no longer just the vehicle for the world to perpetuate itself (cf. Matt 24.36–44). A whole new context is given in which two people now vow to make use of the time that they have promised one another, just as the Church as a whole makes

12 This is a theme explored in Stanley Hauerwas, 2001, 'Sex in Public: How Adventurous Christians Are Doing It', in Berkman, John and Cartwright, Michael (eds), *The Hauerwas Reader*, Durham, NC: Duke University Press, pp. 481–504.

use of the time that remains to witness to the life of the world to come. Indeed, all of our social and kinship relations are relativized and surpass themselves as now a participation in the life of the bride of Christ. Our relationships become intelligible not in the context of state legitimation or 'natural' and cultural needs but in the light of the love of God for his people. The whole of Christian social existence is something enacted anew and performed as a sharing in the love of God and for the sanctification of one another. To quote St John Chrysostom once more:

> But now that resurrection is at our gates, and we do not speak of death, but advance toward another life better than the present, the desire for posterity is superfluous. If you desire children, you can get much better children now, a nobler childbirth and better help in your old age, if you give birth by spiritual labour.[13]

As we have seen, procreation is a good and a good for the Church, but the fruitfulness of human relationships in Christ is not exhausted by procreation. The Christian life does not find its summation in the command 'be fruitful and multiply, and fill the earth and subdue it' (Gen. 1.28) but in the commands to love God, to love our neighbours as ourselves and to love one another as Christ has loved us (Matt. 22.36–40, John 13.34–5). It is in seeing each friend and stranger as a brother, a sister, as a child of God, and as Christ, that we 'get much better children now' (cp. Matt 12.46–50, 25.31–46). Marriage will be fruitful first and foremost when it has taught us how to love others well as part of an intensive schooling sustained over a life-time in the presence of the God who is the giver of the gift of love.

As Paul Fletcher has argued, if we begin to take this idea seriously, then marriage is released from being seen as just a means of perpetuating life in the face of death but a symbol of passion

13 John Chrysostom, 'On the Sacred Institution of Marriage', Homily One, quoted in Davison, Andrew (ed.), 2016, *Amazing Love: Theology for Understanding Discipleship, Sexuality and Mission*, London: Darton, Longman and Todd, p. 48.

in life as a foretaste of the life to come.[14] Therefore our sexual relationships need not be subject to moralistic management or become a contemporary resigned and depthless bacchanalia in the face of impending death, but could truly partake of and stand for a life of ecstatic love. In the face of the pornographic and transitory nature of contemporary erotic entanglements, marriage stands for the time it takes to learn to love and be loved. It points us to the source and spring of that love in the God who is faithful and who, in Jesus, has plighted his troth.

As Fletcher continues, we can then understand marriage (alongside other forms of vowed kinship relationships) as forming part of an alternative Christian economy of good desires and relational practices that challenge and potentially transform the practices and desires formed by late capitalism and contemporary culture. That is, once we recognize that relationships are grounded in the life of God, there is a depth surpassing their merely natural or cultural functions. We begin to see what they are created for and how they, even as also natural and cultural, participate in the divine life and gesture towards the redemption of our social life in Christ.

Marriage becomes an integral part of a whole constellation of renewed and reimagined social relationships by modelling the time it takes to learn how to love. It witnesses to God's love of his people and his world and his promise to fulfil Christ's redeeming work in the age to come. We can see some of the possibilities for a whole ecclesial economy of symbolic relationships including procreative marriages that reveal the Church's need to witness in each new generation, a variety of vowed kinship relationships that witness to the time of learning to love as we await our full common bridal union with Christ, and celibate relationships that exemplify a life lived in community where each disciplines his or her desires in order to focus them on God.[15]

---

14 See Fletcher, Paul, 2007, 'Antimarriage' in Loughlin (ed.), *Queer Theology*, pp. 254–66.

15 This set of ideas is similarly explored in Song, *Covenant and Calling*.

Vows in Troubling Times

Perhaps it is now time to mention some of the elephants in the room. The first is personal. The pledges made in my own marriage did not reach their fulfilment. The breaking down of my marriage brought much hurt and a disordering of lives. And yet, I still hesitate to use a word as final and definitive as 'failure'. The marriage brought forth three wonderful beloved and loving human beings. It included many times that brought joy to us and to others, and has issued in a lasting friendship. God's love is redemptive and by God's grace new joys and opportunities to learn how to love are given even when we fall short.

There will always be very real dangers in idealizing any vowed kinship relationships. There are many marriages that do not feel symbolic of the life to come. Marriages break down. Infidelity is not uncommon. Vows are repeatedly broken as the changes of life (illness, poverty, depression, resentment, loss of passion) put stress on us. There are marriages that are life-denying and painful; marriages in which violence, coercion and rape are present. Partners fall in love with other people even as they remain faithful to their vows (or not). Relationships experienced as more loving and fulfilling are entered upon that strain or break vows. People separate and reunite. A partner may transition or perhaps come to realize that they are gay. And, as I look out at my congregation, I see many people whose marriages have been ended by the parting that comes with death and, for them, the ending of that vowed life means grief and may or may not mean feeling able to enter another relationship.

There will be those for whom being 'released' from marriage vows is something from which they will not recover and those for whom the breaking of the vows in divorce brings an experience of new life, relief and rescue. There is no point sugar-coating the dangers and the hurts. There is no use pretending the vowed life is a panacea or guaranteed to succeed.

Marriage is also put under pressure by consumerism and the contemporary pursuit of novelty. The cultural erosion of values of permanence and life-long commitment take their toll on new generations. There is a preponderance of casual and transient relationships in which sex is seen as something to be consumed and where the partner is the object of an essentially masturbatory gratification in an endless now.[16]

Nevertheless, for each story of marital breakdown, there are many that do speak of the strength of a vowed life in which reconciliation, forgiveness and redemption are *made visible* for others to see. There are sacrifices made that are in the end life-affirming, and endurances undergone that witness to the power and vitality of love.

It is in this context that I find I have a lot of sympathy with those who do not want to 'renew' their vows. My mother – a priest – once met with a couple because the wife wanted to mark an anniversary with a service of renewal of vows. She noticed that the husband seemed taciturn. When she asked him why, he told her that he had already made his vows, he had said them once, he had meant them, and he would let his wife know if anything changed! Nevertheless some of my favourite celebrations are golden and diamond anniversary renewals of vows. A couple stands before you nearer the end than the beginning of the time that they have promised to one another. The fruit of that life can be seen in the fears, griefs and troubles they have lived through together and in the joys, successes and hopes they have shared. They stand there as one flesh, not as two people who could be imagined any longer as not having been one with the other. Probably they still snipe and carp and find themselves annoyed according to well-rehearsed scripts and relate to one another now within the limits of well-ploughed furrows. Yet they witness to a time that has given them the gift of one another in love and, in that, you can see how they have found themselves drawn into the love of God. They have become a sign of a life to come and a sign that, in Christ, *all* of our relationships are being made new.

Perhaps if we can lay hold of the beauty and benefits of vowing to take time to love one another in this vowed affinal kinship relationship that we call marriage, then it might be

16 This prevailing cultural background is also commented on at the opening of the Pilling Report, especially p. xi.

possible for us to learn as a Church that there may well be other forms of vowed kinship relationships that – whether or not we call them marriages – by virtue of being *vowed* can also be understood within the nuptial horizon of the eschatological life of love in which we participate now, but dimly. In so doing, we might better learn how to love one another.

5

Clerical Vows: The 'Wild Choice' of Ordination

JESSICA MARTIN

In this chapter Jessica Martin reflects on how ordination vows within the Church of England, while undergoing significant changes through the various prayer books from the Reformation to today (which she charts here), continue to reflect the necessarily paradoxical ambiguity between what is 'humanly planned' and what is 'divinely authorized'. And yet, although ordination is again founded crucially in baptism, there is something about ordination vows that change the priest into a representative *person, whether s/he likes it or not. The cleric can never be a 'private' person again, but stands in a symbolic realm of Christ's special calling, changed by that very demand.*

'You did not choose me but I chose you.' (John 15.16)

Long ago, over the sea: an episcopal selection process. The brethren have met to choose between a shortlist of candidates. These are men they have already assessed to be competent, fit to wield authority, able, respected, popular – the sort of people you can be really sure will lead their organization well. All that human ingenuity can do to optimize the outcome, to harness the necessary Spirit to imaginable purposes, has been done. It is vital to be conscientious, to be accountable. The only bit left of the discernment process is to put the matter to the vote. Here is Eusebius's account of an astonishing moment in the year 236:

> Several renowned and honourable men were in the minds of many, but Fabian, who was present, was in the minds of none. But they relate that suddenly a dove flying down lighted on his head, resembling the descent of the Holy Spirit on the Savior in the form of a dove. Thereupon all the people, as if moved by one Divine Spirit, with all eagerness and unanimity cried out that he was worthy, and without delay they took him and placed him in the episcopal seat.[1]

So much for process.

Moments of vision, by their nature, are ambiguous. Was the descent of the dove a symbol? a visitation? a re-enactment? a reminder? Eusebius himself is circumspect in his description – this moment *was like* the Holy Spirit descending at Jesus's baptism – and when the people acclaimed Fabian as Pope they were moved '*as if* by one Divine Spirit'. What we do with his inference is our own business. Perhaps Fabian was actually elected because some dumb pigeon's inner radar failed?

Yet even if the dove stooped to alight upon Fabian out of random chance, does that rule the actions of the Holy Spirit out of the count? I don't think so. God breaks into the world like sunshine, the supernatural lighting up the ordinary with wildness, until you cannot be quite sure what you saw, or how you knew it was God visiting. We can neither contain nor predict where the wind will blow, the light fall, the voice speak.

Eusebius's anecdote illustrates a profound tension in the long story of the actions of God upon human beings (and their institutions) in the world: between charism and governance, the reasoned and the untameable, the contingency for which plans must be made and the unexpected for which an attentive space is implored. I want to think about the ways in which ordination sits between the unpredictable and the planned, between the wild, unfathomable choices of God and reasoned human decision-making, both personal and corporate.

Klerus, the Greek word from which the word 'clergy' is derived, first means 'a lot', or 'allotted'.[2] At the buried root of

1 Eusebius, *Historia Ecclesiastica*, 6.29.3–4; quoted in Bradshaw, Paul, 2013, *Rites of Ordination: their History and Theology*, London: SPCK, p. 49.

2 See Bradshaw, *Rites of Ordination*, p. 40.

what makes the clergy, then, is an unexpected alighting which might be random but is also a sacred pointer, as inexplicable as the rationale behind the bizarre, unqualified mixture of men and women who first followed Jesus's call. 'Apostolic' is unpredictable.

Following the call is an out-of-the-blue encounter that falls where it will – wherever God meets a readiness to offer everything within one mixed, fragile and unsatisfactory human soul. But the institutional process leading to ordination requires something else. Ordinands must satisfy the social and professional criteria which they need in order to fulfil the demands of the role – demands which may be very varied indeed in a modern context. Call and competence are not the same thing. And while it is other human beings who make the decisions about competence, the service and the call are God's. His is an 'allotment', a wild choosing, like the choosing of Matthias over another equally qualified candidate in the chance of the lot.[3]

The tension in priesthood between the humanly planned and the divinely appointed has always been there. Nothing will argue it away, because it's not within the reach of reason or subject to our control. The questions asked of ordinands at their ordinations, historically and in the present day, are questions which recognize this and so attempt to reconcile human criteria with divine choice at the culmination of the process. But because that tension *is* there we urgently need to pay attention to the unexpected in seeking to understand the call to ordination and the nature of its vows. And in our own historical moment within Anglican orders the tension is particularly high. This is because in a fast-changing landscape we are not really sure what priesthood either is, or is for; and because there is a move – in part pragmatic – towards lay leadership, for which many of the same skills are key, making a purely competence-based definition of ordination inadequate.

To understand why we are where we are, we need to go back and look at the history of ordination vows and, briefly, at the cultural placing of Church of England clergy. Priestly identity has been a contested field, lying uneasily between ontological and

3 Acts 1.21–26.

functional definitions, certainly since the Church of England was re-defined into a national Church in the 1530s. This was due in part to the jerky and ambiguous relationship between Reformation as it was happening in the rest of Europe, and the different (and much less primarily theological) motivations behind the Act of Supremacy. The currents of reform which moved the Church of England to reduce its sacraments from seven to two, baptism and Holy Communion, also by strong implication reduced ordination from a sacred state in its own right to a cultural function. Ordained ministers might simply be there as a controllable means by which to deliver the benefits of the remaining sacraments, with outworkings of scriptural teaching and pastoral care, to the people. Baptism should be, therefore, the only significant mark of the Holy Spirit's call. In theory. On these lines the Church of England would have followed continental movements to abolish episcopacy and to emphasize a flatter hierarchical structure. But that did not happen.

For in practice it did not work out so neatly. As the German reformers struggled with what ordination was and what priests were for, Martin Bucer produced a Latin version of the Ordinal indebted to their discussions which he offered to Cranmer. Cranmer found it very useful but not definitive.[4] The English Ordinal of 1550 is also heavily indebted to its prominent medieval predecessor, the *Use of Sarum*. Primary features were the litany, the laying on of hands, bidding prayers, consecratory prayers, and the singing of the hymn '*Veni Creator Spiritus*'. The questions and exhortations addressed to ordinands emphasized scripture and scriptural teaching, doctrine and sacraments, study, exemplary holy living, and institutional discipline. All were in *Sarum*. The people were enjoined to pray '*secretly*' (i.e., privately and silently) for the Holy Spirit in all priestly ordinations from 1550 onwards, in words directly translated from *Sarum*, and followed by the '*Veni Creator*', sung in English in the translation still used today.[5] A central aspect of

4 See Bradshaw, Paul, 2007, 'A Brief History of Ordination Rites,' in *Common Worship: Ordination Services, Study Edition*, London: Church House Publishing, p. 118.

5 See Brightman, F. F. (ed.), 1915, *The English Rite*, London: Rivingtons, pp. 988–9.

later medieval ordinations, the 'conferring of elements' (chalice, vestments, etc.) was retained in 1550 and still gestured at vestigially from 1552 in the presentation of a Bible.[6] The increasingly hierarchical understandings of the orders of priesthood characteristic of medieval Christendom[7] also got carried over into their reformed counterparts, and bishops remained key to ecclesiastical polity. The rite existed to marry competences with holiness, vocation with ecclesial obedience and the conferral of an authority which was both sacred and civil. Yet underpinning all of it was the invocation of the Holy Spirit, denoting the unpredictable choice of God and invoked by the prayers of the people.

Every one of these features has remained present in the Ordinal from 1550 to the present day. The theological unease about the precise nature of ordination does not surface in any overt way in either liturgy or vows, though it is discernible in the cautiously separate printing of the Ordinal from the *Book of Common Prayer* between 1550 and 1662, and of course in the banning of the Ordinal (along with *Book of Common Prayer* itself) during the 1640s and 1650s. By the Restoration of the 1660s the explicitly anti-episcopal current of opinion which saw the ordained clergy functionally rather than ontologically had been formally expelled from the Anglican institution and those who favoured this view were founding or supporting the Nonconformist churches. They left behind, though, Anglicans in the reformed Calvinist tradition who for the sake of good ecclesiastical order (rather than on theological grounds) accepted episcopacy, however unenthusiastically; so the tension persisted within as well as without the institution. It remains to this day as a distinctive reformed strand of modern Anglicanism. That is why it is now possible for reformed Anglicans with little taste for the theology underpinning episcopacy to complain on functional grounds if they have no bishop in sympathy with, and thus representative of, their stance.

6 Bradshaw, 'A Brief History', p. 119. Also see Cummings, Brian (ed.), 2011, *The Book of Common Prayer: The Texts of 1549, 1559 and 1662*, Oxford: Oxford World's Classics, pp. 785–6.

7 Bradshaw, 'A Brief History', pp. 116–17.

It is no wonder, then, that modern clergy carry a considerable ambiguity of definition in their persons, both in terms of the sacredness of their office and the nature of their civil standing. This already uncomfortable positioning is much sharpened by our contemporary situation, where we both seek to increase priestly vocation and yet prepare for much lay leadership, and where the civil standing of the clergy has shifted and declined under the pressure of social change. Our reasons for reassessing the lay/clerical relationship, however quick-wittedly they are folded into a laudably fresh theological assessment of priesthood or a necessary re-imagining of our ecclesial relationships, begin from a less exalted place. They are essentially a contingency plan to combat decline and manage ever scarcer resources, a shifting of the ground which attempts to find some purchase on an indifferent world with little ecclesial loyalty to, or knowledge of, its national Church.

Looking at the revisions to the Ordinal which have happened over the last fifty or so years, they can be read as being as much driven by external change as by theological reasoning. Clerical social positioning, both within church communities and in their wider context, seems as significant as debates about ontology. Shifts towards more collaborative models of ministry, with the shared charism of baptism as its rationale, run alongside a new context in which clerical authority is in any case extremely limited. Models of servant leadership represent an admirable option to which – as it happens – there is little alternative. And the setting has changed in other ways. The other meaning of *klerus*, lot or allotment, denotes a piece of land, and the relationship between ministry and place is deep within Anglican clerical identity; but how the clergy belong within a local community – or what a 'local community' even means, for anyone – is currently subject to great change. At this historical moment we are pondering the reducing viability of the parochial system against the vulnerable flexibility of the gathered *ecclesia*, even though our primary scriptural model is mendicant, rootless, as in the challenging commission of Jesus to the seventy disciples,[8]

8 Luke 10.1–12.

still we are profoundly – and systemically – attached to the ancient pairing of place and calling.

The emphasis of this pairing changed in the 1540s. At the dissolution of the monasteries, the *stabilitas* and *caritas* rooting the religious houses gave way to a new aspect of ministry for the ordained parish clergy. The major innovation for the 1550 *Making of Deacons* is a clause for pastoral care and relief: 'it is [the deacon's] ... office to searche for the sycke, poore and impotent people of the parishe ... that ... thei maie be releved by the parishe or other convenient almose'.[9] This marks the beginning of a prominent social and pastoral strand in Anglican orders until the present day – and it quickly comes under the pressure applied by scarce resources. In 1552 the clause 'where provision is so made' is added – and stays. For modern clergy, parish relief in that form is long superseded; but the question of what responsibility the local church might assume for the destitute and the desperate, in a Britain which has ditched universal welfare piecemeal, grows ever more urgent, and becomes a larger and larger element in an increasingly diverse portfolio of clerical and church community activity. Yet as current clergy are asked for more, so they also seem to *belong* less. And at the same time as the social and pastoral aspect of ministry gains a new urgency, churches have become more marginal to localities. We can trace the shift from centre to margin within the modern liturgies.

One tendency, from the ASB onwards, is towards a more private or inward clerical piety. So while a sixteenth- or seventeenth-century deacon was commissioned to read the gospel publicly – 'take thou aucthoritie to read the Gospell in the Churche of God'[10] – a twentieth-century one was exhorted to study the scriptures and pray at home – 'Will you be diligent in prayer, in reading holy Scripture, and in all studies that will deepen your faith and fit you to uphold the truth of the Gospel against error?'[11]

It is true that the earlier declaration was a commissioning, made to accompany the 'elements gift' of a Bible; that in the

9 Brightman, *The English Rite*, p. 988.

10 Brightman, *The English Rite*, p. 953.

11 ASB, p. 345. The same question, in the same words, is asked of priests.

sixteenth-century context 'reading' and 'preaching' are much closer to synonyms (Richard Hooker defines reading as a form of preaching);[12] that literacy was much lower; that all reading was voiced and was not usually seen as a private activity. All the same, the assumptions of the ASB wording seem to be that there is no clear platform from which the Word may be widely proclaimed, and that its proclamation is more likely to be challenging. Public space has become embattled. Someone perhaps noticed this tone in revising the ASB for the *Common Worship* ordination rite, because although the question has been retained, it is immediately balanced by a public and missional question: 'Will you lead your people in proclaiming the glorious Gospel of Christ so that the good news of salvation may be heard in every place?'[13] It is no accident that the question's emphasis on 'leading the people' assumes a shared charism: the clergy may 'lead' but will not be proclaiming the truth of the gospel on their own.

More generally, the modern liturgies show a broadening of professional expectation alongside an ever more liminal vision of clergy presence. Clergy are repeatedly described as inhabiting a space between Church and world, acting as a two-way conduit yet belonging securely in neither place. The language is more missionary, the emphasis is strong for social servanthood, and charisms are characterized wherever possible as shared. In the ASB the very first listing of the deacon's duties presents him as one who works 'with [the Church's] members in caring for the poor, the needy, the sick and all who are in trouble',[14] and the priest is 'sent' and enjoined to 'search for [God's] children in the wilderness of this world's temptations.'[15] Differences between priest and deacon subtly narrow as they become more likely to be ordained together, making the same promises at the same time.

12 Hooker, Richard, *The Laws of Ecclesiastical Polity*, V, 21, 4: 'Our usual public Reading of the word of God for the people's instruction is Preaching.' See http://anglicanhistory.org/hooker/5/5.080-089.pdf (accessed 5 February 2022).

13 *Common Worship: Ordination Services*, p. 62.

14 ASB, 'Ordination of Deacons', p. 370 (combined rite).

15 ASB, 'Ordination of Priests', p. 371 (combined rite).

In the *Common Worship* rite this liminality is very marked; and although deacon and priest are better demarcated, the priest's qualities are also seen as building upon the diaconal. So the deacon is to be a 'herald of Christ's kingdom', as well as bringing 'the needs of the world before the Church in intercession'.[16] Deacons 'watch' for signs of the kingdom and work towards that fulfilment'. Priests also 'watch for the signs of God's new creation' and 'intercede for all in need.'[17] There is a carefully eschatological edge to the language, a pointed distinction between the 'wilderness' of the world and the not-yet-arrived joys of the kingdom for which the people of God watch and work. Yet, while Christians are characterized as a missional minority, the range for clerical engagement with those in need, though vague, appears also to be limitless.

Taken individually, every one of these changes makes theological sense. It does not take *Common Worship*'s scrupulous scriptural referencing for every clause to see that. The Christian, like Christ himself, belongs nowhere, 'for here we have no lasting city, but we are looking for the city which is to come.'[18] For the Christian, it is in our encounters with the sick, the poor and the stranger that we recognize, and are recognized by, the Lord of life.[19] Baptism with the Holy Spirit is indeed the foundational scriptural sign for Christian transformation, and the systems and hierarchies worked out by the early Church, as we read of them in the New Testament, are much more ambiguously marked. We do indeed look towards the kingdom that is coming as a night-watcher looks for the signs of the morning.[20] The 'neighbour' parable of the good Samaritan points out that limited sacred communities cannot police their borders if they wish truly to participate in the generosity of God's love.[21]

However, an unintended effect of combining shared, baptismally based ministry, a social and pastoral outreach emphasis,

16 *Common Worship: Ordination Services*, p.15.
17 *Common Worship: Ordination Services*, p.7.
18 Hebrews 13.14.
19 See Matthew 25.31–46.
20 See Psalm 130.6.
21 See Luke 10.25–37.

the proliferation of roles, and an emphasis on the liminally missionary, is inevitably to de-emphasize in proportion the exclusively 'churchy' duties of the ordained in relation to the sacraments, preaching and the occasional offices. It's not that these are declared to be less important. It's simply that they are jostled by a larger volume of other requirements. The effect is rather like – and perhaps is – a proliferating role description which has gained its add-ons in an attempt to combine and adjust different models of what the role means. At the same time as the defined priestly duties of the 'Christendom' model persist – with their cumbersome administrative structures belonging to a different world – so a new set of definitions spring up on a generous and demanding 'Kingdom' model, which sees no committed social activity as beyond the bounds and competence of the trained priest.

The influential radical movement within the Church from the early 1960s onwards campaigned for social action, often in explicit opposition to the maintenance of church institutions. It was very successful, both in its influence on different aspects of social justice movements, and in its zeal to decrease the social reach and influence of the institutional Church. We have inherited the emphasis and commitment to social justice, but we also inherited a Church which used its influence publicly to repudiate its institutional presence. The pews emptied. Consequently we find that we attempt to alleviate the world's ills assisted by ever tinier and more elderly handfuls of committed churchgoers. Our ordination rites stress our care for the sick, the poor and the desperate. Yet neither priest nor deacon may be professionally equipped or well placed to offer it well; and if they are it will not be as a result of their ordination training.[22] It is perhaps no accident that so many priests coming to ordination after another professional career have had (or

22 See Brewitt-Taylor, Sam, 2018, *Christian Radicalisation in the Church of England and the Invention of the British Sixties, 1957–1970*, Oxford: OUP. Brewitt-Taylor traces the extent to which a readiness to see God working in the world had its corollary in a readiness to neglect or abandon the care of the Church, in ways which paralleled, encouraged and speeded up the loss of church commitment in the nation at large. 12% of Anglican clergy ordained between 1951 and 1965, he reports, had left the Church by 1973 (p. 226). Anticipatory logic is not always our friend.

continue to have alongside their priesthood) backgrounds in teaching, social work, law, and the NHS. Losing the status of establishment, we nevertheless commit ourselves to taking the strain of the failures of the state to which we are aligned.[23]

So what are priests for? What makes an ordained person any different from a leader of community or a dismally unqualified volunteer social worker? On moving from an academic post to parish ministry I tried to tell a former colleague what it was I now did all day. She listened politely, sceptically. Perhaps I explained badly. After a pause she said – 'Yes, but you do hand over the stuff you encounter pastorally to *professionals*, don't you?' (For even ten years ago it was more possible to imagine that there were professionals available to whom cases could be handed over than it is today.) I have thought about it often since; and about the needy circumstances with which I have been involved – often those points beyond intervention, the dying person for whom nothing can be done except being there, the bereaved, the despairing, the lonely, the neglected frail. I think about it now as I regularly encounter men and women in mental torment whose suffering I am absolutely unequipped to understand or tackle. But I know also that *action* is not only, perhaps even not primarily, what I am a priest for.

What about being – and becoming? Prayer, study, teaching, presence? What makes an ordained person any different from any other baptized member of God's Church? The life of prayer and witness, the service of the gospel: these are the charisms of every person who has turned to Christ. What are the ordained to be, to become, or to do, beyond the fulfilment through grace of their baptismal promises? Will it be found in a skill-set, or in leadership potential, or in emotional intelligence, or in community commitment? All these may be necessary, but are they sufficient? What makes a priest?

23 Archbishop Justin Welby's (2018) *Reimagining Britain: Foundations for Hope*, London: Bloomsbury, gambles on establishment still having enough social reach for the Anglican social justice commitment to win back souls for Christ. The vision has been, rightly, compared to Archbishop Temple's post-war welfare achievements; but whereas Temple could use the Church of England's social ascendancy to transform Britain systemically, Archbishop Welby has to point to the patchwork of care and commitment which churches offer as a reason for the state to take any notice of Christianity at all.

The history of ordination vows from earliest times to the present day will not tell you the answer, or at least not definitively. There was, it appears, never a time when the nature of ordained ministry – or its relationship to the calling of all the baptized – was established beyond doubt. On the contrary, its history will chart the uneasy lurch between charism and institutional stability, between ontology and functionalism, as well as between serving with and serving for, between representative and collective offerings back to God of the gifts of life. 'The breaking of bread and the prayers' are not, initially, sacerdotal but hospitable: only as the meal becomes formalized into a sacrificial rite aside from *agape* is that link made. Teaching and study are not necessarily primary for the early Church's ministers: the fair distribution of alms may be at least as important. Ordinations before the third century are made by, and out of, the body of the baptized faithful. In the eyes of many (famously, St John Chrysostom), word is as central as sacrament in the understanding of priestly identity.[24]

These tensions between inspiration and institution can't be separated out to reveal a buried narrative of the right way to do things (though that has certainly been tried). You can't, for example, read the Spirit as always athwart the tendency to human organization or even to human hierarchy (though that, too, has been tried). Some doves really are only dumb pigeons. Some popular votes really are disaster. Those early shared meals were in people's houses, when the one presiding was likely to be the householder (and so, from what we know of the earliest Church, as likely to be a woman as a man) and the meals were real meals – how inspiring that is – until you read Paul's first letter to the early Church in Corinth and realize that without regulation it could degenerate into a cliquey, drunken party of unequals.[25] One way of understanding the earliest institution of the office of bishop is neither as a theologian (a few

24 John Chrysostom's homily given on the day that he was ordained priest (*Sermo cum presbytero fuit ordinatus*), cited in Bradshaw, *Rites of Ordination*, p. 45. See, e.g., section 1, where he cites Hosea 14.2 and Psalm 69.30–31: https://www.tertullian.org/fathers/chrysostom_first_sermon.htm (accessed 5 February 2022).

25 See 1 Corinthians 11.17–22.

were illiterate[26]) nor a saint, but as a competent overseer and manager who would legislate for what was normative, check the messianic tendencies of those of his band of prophets who had let the power of persuasion go to their heads, make sure that resources were distributed fairly, and generally maintain the institution's stability. The maintenance of good discipline is central to the vows a bishop makes at ordination.[27]

This is not a cop-out, nor a betrayal of the Spirit; indeed, speaking as someone who was chewed up and spat out by a noxious house church in my teens, I think that without ecclesiological structure and accountability we will damage more people than we will nurture. We have our gifts of discernment, of assessment, of planning, for a reason – and though they betray us, they do so when we forget how they are governed by the two Great Commandments. When, that is, we treat our gifts as fully usurping the place where we listen and watch for the unpredictable will of God, and when we attempt to substitute those gifts for all the risky human acts of trust. (For, yes, maintaining the institution can – does – will in the future – miss, constrain, attempt to silence the Spirit speaking from the margins. We are not in the kingdom of heaven yet.)

What we want of priesthood remains ill-defined, sitting between, on the one hand, what can be planned for, discerned and fostered, and on the other a holiness, a connection to the Person of God, traceable to an unquantifiable encounter between God and the self which we call 'vocation', or 'calling'. Yet, in the case of the ordained, this calling is in some sense distinct from (as well as dependent upon) the foundational baptismal call. We recognize intellectually that many callings are not to priesthood; but, given our primary focus on eucharistic worship since the Parish Communion movement, this is often a lip-service belied in our readiness to shove anyone who shows a spark of leadership potential along with their vocation into ordination training. The practical impact of the ubiqui-

26 See Bradshaw, *Rites of Ordination*, p. 48; Stewart-Sykes, Alistair (ed.), 2006, *The Apostolic Church Order*, Strathfield, NSW: St Paul's Publications, pp. 60–2.

27 'The Ordination and Consecration of a Bishop' in *Common Worship: Ordination Services*, p. 61, para. 3.

tous weekly Eucharist on the nature of ecclesial community, its doubtful capacity for welcoming and absorbing those who do not yet have any faith, its effect on the nature and function of the priesthood within lived Anglicanism: these are issues we view uneasily, frequently, and without consensus.

Within the Fresh Expressions/Pioneer nexus the non-sacramental options are being explored: lots of cafés, shared meals, hospitality-with-teaching. We are rediscovering the *agape* meal – and noticing that we do not need priests for that task. All we need is training. Training in competences, even training in holiness. If ordination is just a kind of institutional extra, an optional and ontologically insignificant add-on to the foundational death-and-resurrection rite of baptism which brought us into the household of faith, there's a beautiful clarity to the position. It places ministers within the baptismal family rather than setting them apart; it is altogether a higher and more demanding concept of what it might be to be the whole people of God; it allows for a more collaborative model of ministry; it is a wholesome corrective to the clerical tendency to be uppity. The vision is noble. Its logic should include lay presidency and structures which decouple holiness and hierarchy. So why does it feel as if it has missed something out? – as if something of the wild light of the crazy divine selection process has been legislated away?

The Church of England has refused a couple of opportunities radically to shift its ordination vows so as to reflect the baptismal, non-ontological model for ordination: before 1550, and at the turn of this century in preparing *Common Worship*. Each time, the reasons weren't exactly theological. In the 1540s the authorities wanted as much continuity as possible with the Latin rite; in our own day those devising the *Common Worship* rite, having formed their own vows upon the older ASB version which itself is deeply indebted to the BCP, found themselves reluctant to tinker with the instruments of their own formation.[28] This is probably wisdom, but of the instinctive rather than the reasoned kind, rather in the way cathedrals survived

28 Bradshaw, *Rites of Ordination*, pp. 191–213, and anecdotally from Dr. Bridget Nichols (Church of Ireland Theological Institute) in relation to *Common Worship*.

by a series of fond accidents, or Augustine was kinder about music than about the other creative arts because Milanese psalmody played a part in his conversion.[29]

There are practical drawbacks, however, to the 'it's all just baptism really' approach, just as there is to the perfect reformed logic of saying there are no special days in the year but Sunday. The 'priesthood of all believers' vision of the Church implicitly requires us to valorize a gathered membership, to exclude the sleeping partners, the 'culturally baptized'. We cannot quantify the loss of this because we have not succeeded in doing it yet. Yet, insofar as we still have a platform from which to speak truth to power, it is the cultural platform of Establishment with its thousands upon thousands of well-intentioned, sleeping church members, the people who come to the Christingle and the carol service, to funerals and weddings, who baptize their children knowing full well they won't be back until the next cultural milestone, the next carol service. We can't read from baptism to the visible outworking in commitment, but we rely more than we acknowledge on the hinterland to give us a missional platform.

If we treat ordination as only functional, we blur the difference between offering somebody a deeper experience of the disciplines of holiness and training them as an organizational leader. If ordination is functional we have to ignore all the inchoate, yet deeply powerful ways in which the call to ordination really does bring about for those undergoing it an absolute change, a profound re-orientation into being a particular vehicle for the work of God. This is not simply about a leadership role. It is about being subdued and distilled into the rest of your vowed life by the spirit of discipline your vows require. It is saying that your primary duty is to be holy for God. That should be the prayer and aim for every baptized person, and for some it is; yet for the ordained there is an extra bit, an exemplary visibility for various reasons played down in the narrative of modern formation, but profoundly important. The priest is not a private person. The symbolic representation of Christ's role (performed in sacramental presidency but

29 See Augustine, *Confessions*, 10.33.

equally demanding in the most trivial of everyday exchanges and vital in preaching and teaching) changes the persons taking it on. They cease to exist for themselves. 'For I think God has exhibited us ... as though sentenced to death, because we have become a spectacle to the world, to angels and to mortals.'[30] Clergy *represent*, in a character which is not our own but Christ's, not choosing but chosen, painfully and deliberately visible.

Augustine had a phrase for this re-shaping of the self as exemplary spectacle, the *character dominicus*, the nature or stamp of the Lord. The medieval Church was enormously interested in this notion of witnessing 'characters' to holiness; and the post-Reformation Church follows its lead in its stress on clergy and bishops as 'godly examples and patterns'.[31] The clerical life is set apart as a continual living witness to the teaching, healing, dying and rising presence of Christ. In one sense, it does nothing else; every promise is subordinated to this end. Just as Chrysostom claimed, so the whole preaching and teaching, studying and reading in the service of the gospel, are elements of sacred character covered in the range of promises and affirmations made in both the Latin and English rites from the medieval Church and up to the present day.

Clergy are representative, but they are not uniform. The variety of those called (though not as great as it could be if our own spiritual imaginations, along with the doors we keep, were wider) is always breathtaking, life-giving. Many say they could not believe or understand why God called them, actually them (rather than the ordination-clone in their heads) with the muddle of their lives and histories bumping along behind them: baggage to be transformed into the resources of wisdom. It is never all planning. We are alighted upon by divine chance, in a world of contingency. We come out of the world which shaped our growing for this purpose: in order to reflect back to it through the spectacle of our selves how its chaos might become a wilder beauty.

30 1 Corinthians 4.9.

31 Brightman, *The English Rite*, p. 984.

6

Religious Vows: 'The Liberty to Bind'

SR JUDITH, SLG

Sr Judith, SLG returns in this chapter to the contentious nature of the Religious vows that originally disturbed Anglican sensibilities in the nineteenth century when Religious life was revived in the Church of England (see Chapter 1). Were these vows somehow threatening to the status quo *of political and erotic life in the nation at large? Would any failure in celibate vows therefore somehow signal also a threat to the vows of marriage? Focusing again on the foundational role of baptismal vows for all vows that are built upon them (in this case those of the Religious life), Sr Judith here re-explores the deep Augustinian paradox of the relation of apparently restrictive disciplines to the emergence of true freedom-in-Christ. The demands, and the inevitable pain, involved in Religious obedience to a Rule is – when rightly understood and practised – a means of true freedom: freedom-in-God rather than freedom-from-God. And this admittedly counter-cultural insight has profoundly corporate as well as individual significance – for the world as well as for the Church. Coming full circle, then, we may see this insight as the secret fruit of all the Christian vows, but one that Religious vows may particularly display to a wider culture of simultaneous scepticism and spiritual fascination.*

Christmas morning in my early twenties saw me at the local hospice playing my violin for their service. Just before it began a very anxious lady was wheeled in next to me. The nurse who brought her in reassured her that she would stay with her throughout the service and work the suction machine (one rather like you find in a dentist when you are having work done), as she was suffering from motor neurone disease and having trouble swallowing. At Communion the chaplain broke off the tiniest corner of a wafer and gave it to her saying, 'the Body of Christ', and then added so gently, 'just suck it Meg, it will dissolve', as did all her anxiety.

That brief encounter lodged with me and left me thinking: that is what I want to do with my life; let it dissolve so it brings Christ to people. The means I have chosen, or perhaps that chose me, is to live under vows as a Religious, in my case through the vows of poverty, chastity and obedience. (The vows do differ slightly between different Orders, some taking vows of conversion of life and stability). 'Dissolve' does not imply annihilation here, note, since when salt dissolves in water it doesn't cease to be, but rather changes state from being a solid to being dissolved and making all the water salty. I hope that my life lived under vows is a means by which Christ becomes more present in the world. Perhaps one could say that this is a means of 'incarnation'? I change my 'state' of a single person living her own individual life, to being a person who is bound by the vows of Religious profession and living in community, trusting that that offering is the means to 'free' me to be the most human being that I am created to be, and that for the world this brings Christ to bear on it. The vows don't dissolve me in the sense of destroying me; they free me to become my true self made in the image of God and to live, perhaps at a distance from the ordinary norms of society, precisely in order to engage with it at a different level. Or to borrow the image Augustine himself uses of the Eucharist, we become what we eat, Christ infusing us and ultimately bringing us to the full-stature of himself. Professing the vows of Religious life is a catalyst in that process. Vows, it has been said, create community: the community of the baptized which is the Church; the community which is society and which marriage vows support by uniting two families and more; the community of the Church which the vows of ordination sustain; and the community of those seeking their freedom-in-God in service of the world and who usually live together in a Religious community who by their vows commit their relationship to God and one another.

The basis of all the Religious vows are the baptismal vows. That is actually expressed in what female members of Religious orders wear. Before they take their vows they usually wear a white veil – white representing their baptismal vows. When they make their vows the colour of the veil changes, usually to black to represent the overshadowing of Mary by the Holy Spirit – something which is rich in resonances of Christ being formed in us, and also in our imitation of Mary who is seen to be the archetype of the Religious life. But if you look closely, the black veil is still worn over something white. At the ceremony of making vows the black veil is placed over the white one, symbolically representing the fact that the foundation of the Religious vows are the baptismal vows. The white that remains visible after the black veil is worn is a continual reminder of those baptismal vows and, in certain practical designs such as the one I currently wear, the black veil is actually *secured* on my head by the white cap. Indeed this was so important to me that I chose to re-new my baptismal vows on the morning of the service I made my Religious ones. For me the first question of the renewal of baptismal vows summed it all up: 'Do you turn to Christ?' In one way the Religious life is quite simply a structure for 'turning to Christ' with all your life, an intensification of baptism which leads to a particular way of living. Making Religious vows is a radical and unusual thing to do, but if baptism is taken seriously they make perfect sense.

The title of this chapter ('The Liberty to Bind') comes from the service at which I first professed those vows, and it is deliberately provocative, especially in the twenty-first century when relinquishing control, the ownership of things, and the chance of a sexual relationship, is usually interpreted as the exact opposite of liberty, and when 'binding' is seen as dangerous and toxic rather than freeing. What I hope to do is demonstrate how being 'bound' actually sets you free, which is the whole purpose of the vows. Right at the beginning of the form of profession the sister is asked: 'What do you desire?' (a question that is asked in other forms of vows too). And she answers:

'The mercy of God and liberty to bind myself to him in this community in a life of prayer and reconciliation to his honour and glory.' This liberty is entering into a way of *being*; it may, to be sure, curtail some freedom to *do* certain things, just as the vows of marriage curtail the freedom to do certain things. But it engenders a lifetime of a particular relationship to God and to those who have also made their vows in the community, which in turn brings into being the full person the vowed Religious was created to be: liberty indeed! The form of profession mirrors that answer by now requiring the one to be professed to say:

> I, *N* [Sister Judith of the Mercy of God] do make my Profession and do bind myself to Almighty God, the Father, the Son and the Holy Ghost, in the presence of blessed Mary, Mother of our Lord Jesus Christ and all the whole company of heaven, of you Reverend Father and of all here present, to live under the Vows of Poverty, Chastity and Obedience for one year/the rest of my life,[1] according to the Rule and Constitution of the Community of the Sisters of the Love of God.

After making that Profession publicly the sister is given the signs of that profession: a black veil and a girdle with three knots, one knot for each vow. The girdle is given to her with the words: 'Receive this girdle. As you are bound to Christ, so in him you are free.'

This freedom is something that is grown into all through one's life. The best image I have for it is the magnetizing of a metal strip. If you stroke a piece of metal with a magnet all the atoms in the metal strip begin to align themselves with the orientation of the magnet until the metal strip itself is magnetized. The vows work on the person taking them just as the magnet works on the metal atoms in the strip, and aligns the person to Christ.

1 When vows are first taken they are taken only for a temporary period of one year. After temporary vows have been made for three years a sister may ask to make vows for life. See Chapter 7 on the historical background to temporary and permanent vows.

The formal Questions asked of a sister and the consecratory blessing given to her when she makes her Life Vows and is consecrated as a Religious begin to give a hint of how Religious are 'set free' by their vows. The questions are:

> Do you promise to live in complete dependence on Christ through the Vow of Poverty?
> Do you promise to dedicate every faculty of body, mind and spirit to his service through the Vow of Chastity?
> Do you promise to unite your will with the will of God within this Community through the Vow of Obedience?

And the corresponding blessings are:

> Grant that she may live by faith, rooted in hope, loving the whole world with a never-failing charity.
> Grant her a heart that is poor and hungers for your righteousness and peace.
> Grant her humility and purity of heart, singleness of purpose and a burning love for you.
> Grant that in silence, solitude and prayer she may discover you in the depths of her heart.
> Lead her into that interior wilderness where she may grow in the spirit of obedience and sacrifice, so that purified by the joys and sorrows of this life she may know that perfect love which casts out fear.

The first of those blessings really sums up being given the liberty to receive the adoption God creates for us in Christ (see Rom. 8.15–17). Children generally take after their parents, and as Hebrews describes the Son: 'He is the reflection of God's glory and the exact imprint of God's very being, and he sustains all things by his powerful word' (1.3), so that we are called to grow into the likeness of Christ. When I was dithering about the rights and wrongs of joining a contemplative order that did no active good work, I was asked the question: 'Does this sort of life increase your compassion?' A few days earlier I had found myself in town late at night waiting at a bus stop and watching a man sitting on a pub doorstep all by himself drinking yet another pint (he had several empties beside him) and rather than experiencing my usual fear and impatience with heavy drinking I found myself with a very sorrowful heart thinking: 'I wonder what pain he is trying to cover up?' Although that was twenty-five years ago I still remember that man and my ability to answer the compassion question easily with a 'yes', which was part of what enabled me to undertake trying this way of life. It is much harder to trace *how* it works, how this contemplative life gives rise to an increase in compassion, but I can witness to the fact that it does. It is probably through the silence which reveals my own inner hurts, fears, irritations, coping mechanisms, alongside the patience, presence, persistence, compassion and mercy of God that my own compassion slowly grows. That insight really leads on to the next two blessings which relate to the vow of poverty.

Poverty is not only about material things, though it is concretely about them – not owning them and them not possessing you. But it is also about our inner poverty: what the blessing refers to as humility. One desert father's answer to the question, 'what do you do in the monastery all day?' was, 'we get up and fall down, get up and fall down'; and that is a good description. We are not perfect, and we all fall daily. What we *do* do is learn how to get up, how to let go of the desire to be perfect and not to mind so much about the falling but to rejoice in the repeated opportunity of experiencing mercy and finding the mercy of God to be the place in which we stand. Thus we learn to live in complete dependence on Christ, both on his mercy and for his giving us our meaning and all that we need – which may not be anything like what we *think* we need. In today's materialist society it is easy to think that what we have or can control gives us our meaning; poverty slowly teaches us otherwise. The repeated experience of our own falling, our own need and our need of others, is the soil in which compassion can grow.

Linked to that insight and that increase in compassion is the vow of Chastity. I find it best put by Fr Martin Smith in a piece he wrote about the late Donald Allchin who looked

> to the deepest core of the monastic identity: a call to undergo an inner unification – to become *monos*, single in heart – that stretched and deepened our capacity for solidarity with a broken world, and a costly, empathic participation in its reconciliation at the deepest level of prayer. He took Evagrius's definition of the monk 'separated from all and united to all' and made it not a slogan for an exotic elite, but a mirror in which each Christian could see that she or he was called to be, again in Evagrius's words 'one who thinks of himself as one with all because he unceasingly thinks he sees himself in everyone'.[2]

My post-Nuremberg generation was brought up with the notion that we had to question what anyone in authority asked us to do. Simply 'obeying orders' without thinking about whether what we were being asked to do was right was not acceptable or justifiable, and quite rigorously opposed. Furthermore, the erosion of trust in authority following revelations of MPs' expenses scandals and abuse by priests and nuns renders obedience to be possibly the most suspect of the vows today. Yet it comes from the Latin word which at its heart is the word for listening. What obedience asks of us is to *listen* to God, to listen for God in every circumstance, person and situation. This can often demand of us a temporary silencing of our own ideas and a will and a patience and stillness that allows God to come through. Thus our wills become 'one energy with the will of God', as our Rule puts it, and we become paradoxically freer to be ourselves and to act in accordance with God's will. As the post-Communion collect for feasts of Mary puts it: 'We thank you that in this sacrament of our redemption you visit us with your Holy Spirit and overshadow us by your power; strengthen us to walk with Mary the joyful path of obedience and so to bring forth the fruits of holiness.'[3]

2 Evagrius 'On Prayer', 124–5. Cited in Smith, Martin L., 2015, 'Solitude and Communion: Donald Allchin as Interpreter of the Monastic Vocation and the Mystery of Personhood', in Keller, David G. R. (ed.), *Boundless Grandeur: The Christian Vision of A.M. (Donald) Allchin*, Cambridge: James Clarke, pp. 111–21, at p. 114.

3 2000, *Common Worship: Services and Prayers for the Church of England*, London: Church House Publishing, p. 439.

My most costly living out of obedience came, as is so often the case, almost immediately after I had made my first vows. My best friend, whom I had known from the age of seven and who was a fellow musician, was suddenly diagnosed with liver cancer nine days after the birth of her second child. She lived at the time in Hong Kong, but was advised to return immediately to Scotland where she had made her family home. She was passing through Heathrow, and having been given only two weeks to live I thought seeing her there was my last chance to see her at all. I asked if I could go and was told 'no'. Had I not been bound by vows I would simply have walked out on the spot. To me our friendship and the humanness of saying 'goodbye' were paramount, and surely God would think so too?! The person who said 'no', however, was also listening to God and the needs of the whole community. I was allowed to phone my friend fortnightly and when, after she had undergone some chemotherapy, three months later I again asked if I could go and see her then, as her son was being baptized and she was reportedly getting weaker, I was given permission to go. I travelled up to Scotland, and had the strange gift of being there when she died. Being with the family at that time, as well as being there for myself, is something I deeply treasure in memory. And so in this case the story of obedience bore its fruit.

But obedience can of course also be abused. It is tremendously difficult to hear and enact it aright, especially if you are the person asking obedience and when you have many different circumstances to take into consideration. But in this case (even though during those three months I would have sworn that I was wrongly being prevented from visiting my friend) I believe that God led the one asking obedience and this conspired to bring good out of the situation. In less striking ways that kind of listening for yourself to what you hear God asking, and having that checked and balanced by others and circumstances, can hone our wills to be obedient to God and is one of the great blessings of community – but nonetheless it has to be admitted that it can also be one of its dangers.

The outward sign of consecration as a Religious is usually a ring. Some communities wear their rings on their left hand like a marriage ring; others, like my own, wear the ring on their right hand indicating a difference between marriage vows and Religious consecration. The words said to us as we receive the ring are: 'Receive this ring as a sign of your consecration and of the covenant of faithful and eternal love between you and your Lord.' I have to confess I have always thought that should be the other way round, that is, 'between your Lord and you', since the instigator of the covenant is most definitely God. My part is but a response to God's faithful love, a 'frail echo of the unbreakable promise and commitment of God to humanity' as Petà Dunstan puts it in Chapter 7 (below). The outward sign is significant because it witnesses to the vows to the people of God and that faithfulness of God which is towards all people. The vows are something I as an individual make, but they are not only for my sake. They are made for the Church and for the world. The eleventh-century Benedictine Peter Damian expressed it well when he said:

> Indeed we who are many are one in Christ, each of us possess the whole and so in our bodily solitude we seem to be far from the Church, yet we are most immediately present through the inviolable mystery of unity. And so it is that that which belongs to all belongs to each, and conversely that which is particular to some is common to all in the unity of faith and love.[4]

It follows that my vows are not only my business, but the business of the whole Church, a gift for the Church, a witness and a reminder of the deep seriousness of baptism; and for that reason Religious vows are witnessed by a Bishop on behalf of the Church. The ring serves to remind me too, on bad days and in difficult patches, both that I am bound (to steady me to persevere), and also of the faithful and eternal love of God which has drawn me. Like marriage, the Religious vows serve to witness to God's love, relationship and faithfulness, and life under them helps us to learn to love and be loved. Although life

4 Damian, Peter, 1959, *Selected Writings on the Spiritual Life*, translated by Patricia McNulty, London: Faber and Faber, pp. 63–4.

in community can be hard and frustrating, I continue to be held in my Religious vows by the fact that ultimately when I made my vows I believed that this was the way God was promising to be faithful to *me*. It was the way of life in which God had promised to be for me 'for the rest of my life' (it having taken seven years of testing prior to taking life vows); and my making vows was, first and foremost, a response to that faithfulness, the faithfulness of God. While it can be tempting to get out of a difficult situation, I do not leave or ask for release from these vows, as to do so would call into question God's faithfulness. (Admittedly, as with most vows there is a mechanism for being released from Religious vows just as there is one for being released from marriage vows in very unhappy or extreme circumstances.)[5] Nonetheless, my original vows mean that I have to trust when things are difficult that God *is* there, active and working and always will be; and the vows also require me to realize that difficulties are not an indication of God's absence, which can be a tempting way to resolve the tension of the difficulty. The reducing numbers of those in Religious vows and the demise of some communities can indeed make some anxious about the future of Religious life in general, and certainly communities always need to review whether their way of life truly reflects the radical call of the gospel expressed in their vows. But whether or not I am the last person left alive to have taken those vows in the context of my own community, until I die I believe that God's faithfulness will be there for me. It will be there too for any who choose to live this way of life; and looking at the history of Religious life over the centuries it has always gone through ups and downs. In England there were even three centuries of its non-existence after the Reformation; yet as Petà Dunstan's reflections in this book show there is something vital about it which makes this demanding form of life ultimately inextinguishable. I would suggest part of the reason for that is the equally inextinguishable faithfulness of God, as well as the call in the human heart which leads to Religious life in various forms, not only in the Christian tradition.

5 This problem is addressed at greater length in the Introduction to this volume, and its historical importance for the history of revived Anglican Religious life is discussed in Chapter 1, above.

Poverty, chastity and obedience do fly in the face of contemporary Western society's preoccupation with wealth, success and power; yet they offer an alternative model and a remarkable route for human flourishing. Over time they hopefully 'dissolve' me so that Christ is carried to the Church and to the world. So, to repeat: I am 'bound' by my Religious vows; 'bound' (as in 'my destination is') for freedom; 'bound' to God ('whose service is perfect freedom', as the second collect at morning prayer in the *Book of Common Prayer* puts it so beautifully); and 'bound' to that same faithfulness which has bound itself to me through the history of salvation. And so *what* I 'desire' (as I was asked at my profession) is to grow in that liberty, that way of being, until finally I *become* what I desire – I become one with the mercy of God itself.

PART II

Contemporary Anglican Reflections on the 'Vowed Life' of Religious Community

7

Religious Vows in the Church of England, Then and Now

PETÀ DUNSTAN

In her second contribution to this volume, the historian of Anglican Religious history Petà Dunstan turns back to provide a brief history of how Religious vows in the Church of England originated and developed, how they were initially debated nationally, and how a new interest in them has developed in recent decades. She reflects on what this resurgence bespeaks, and on how 'old' and 'new' Religious vows and forms of life may need to interrelate in order to regenerate the life of the Church in this complex, post-modern, generation.

On 6 June 1841, a young woman in Oxford took vows of religion in the house of her parish priest, before going to the University Church to receive Communion at the Eucharist. It was a momentous personal step for the 24-year-old Marian Hughes, but it was also a significant development for her Church, for Marian was an Anglican. These were the first 'public' Religious vows taken by a member of the Church of England since the Reformation. At its simplest, a vow is a promise made to God, a promise anyone can make at any time. When private, it remains a matter of conscience and prayer for the person making the vow. But when the vow is made to the church, before a priest or bishop, it is a 'public' vow and thereby has a wider significance.

What were the roots of this significance? Reviving Religious life was one fruit of the Tractarian or Oxford movement, begun in the 1830s, whose leaders sought to recall the Church of England to what they saw as the catholic elements of its heritage. They did so in order to revive the Church of England and defend it against what they rejected as liberal views that were taking hold both in theology and political life. One element of this catholic 'defence' was the restoration of Religious vows, often referred to as the 'evangelical counsels' of poverty, chastity and obedience. (Benedictine vows have a different formula, but similar commitments, with the addition of a vow of stability and 'conversion of life'.)

As considered in an earlier chapter of this book (Chapter 1), the revival of Religious communities also gained impetus from social conditions and the need for the Church to deal with the pastoral and welfare problems that arose from industrialization and rapid urbanization. The question of vows therefore was not seen as central to that revival by many beyond the communities: the works and ministries were what mattered. However, to the Religious themselves, the true pioneers of the revival, the vows were central. Without that public commitment to God, their life of sacrifice would be insufficiently anchored. It would be the equivalent to them of two people living together as spouses without the vow of marriage.

Yet the vows for Religious were a controversial matter for reasons other than theology. The Oxford movement was associated with opposition to the government's plans to impose changes on the Church of Ireland and the increasing influence over the established church of non-Anglicans. Anything associated with the tractarian position, such as the revival of Religious life, was seen as linked to a political campaign. Some tractarians became disillusioned with the failure of the Church to be freed from this political interference, and left Anglicanism for the Roman Catholic Church, most famously, John Henry Newman. This unfortunately associated all things tractarian with another strong prejudice in British society: anti-Catholicism.

Britain's enemies for over three hundred years had been 'Catholic powers', notably Spain and then France, and in the 1840s it was only three decades since the country had fought a long and dangerous campaign against revolutionary and then

Napoleonic France. In the popular imagination, monks and nuns were inextricably linked to 'papism' and consequently a danger to the country. Ironically, the French Revolution's persecution of monastics had led many to flee to Britain for refuge, and toleration for Religious life had increased. But this reaction was temporary and by the 1850s anti-Catholic prejudice was rife once more. All Anglicans who took vows therefore risked a backlash from their contemporaries.

This context made the matter a headache for the bishops. As communities began to be founded in the late 1840s and 1850s, the status of vows became contentious. Religious wanted bishops to receive their vows; bishops wanted to avoid being associated with them. It is important to note here, however, that the revival of community life itself was not the problem for the bishops, any more than for the clergy. Many encouraged the founding of Religious communities to provide a group of helpers in parishes for social work and mission. They understood the link between prayer and service that a Religious community represented. Indeed, the Bishop of London even founded a community himself in 1848. Crucially, however, he insisted that the sisters in it did not take vows, precisely illustrating that it was the vows that caused the difficulties for him.[1]

The problem of the vows was essentially their permanence – the life commitment. Bishops and other influential clergy understood this crucial element very well, and fretted over their status. If the vows were private promises then it was unnecessary to have a bishop or a priest present when they were taken. However, if they were public, valid and binding – like marriage vows – then they were indissoluble. In the 1840s, marriage vows could only be set aside by an Act of Parliament; and even when, in the late 1850s, divorce became possible through the courts, it was an expensive and socially perilous action for any individual to pursue.

What would happen if a life-vowed Anglican Religious left their Religious house and refused to return? What if the Religious then tried to get married? Were they to be pursued as

1 The community was the Nursing Sisters of St John the Divine, and its members refrained from taking Religious vows until the 1920s.

criminals as a bigamist would be? Would this be a civil criminal offence or something for an ecclesiastical court? The implications were immense. In the anti-Catholic atmosphere of the time, it was well-nigh impossible to envisage getting anything through parliament on the matter. Bishops understandably therefore felt that it was better to 'leave well alone' and not acknowledge Religious vows in any form other than as private promises.

The tussle over vows became a long unresolved tension and created the myth that bishops were against Religious life itself, and that Religious were 'martyrs' in the Anglo-catholic cause. It was long-lasting as a perception, but the nub of the problem was somewhat hidden as a result. What we have to note is that for the Religious, the vows were the 'call'; the community life and the particular ministry were a consequence of those vows. There were many avenues through which people of faith could serve their neighbours without vows. For Marian Hughes and those who followed her, the Religious life was not about ministry as such: it was about a relationship with God that would be a witness to the Church and the world around them. Marian herself originally envisaged a hidden contemplative community, and only in the 1850s did she adjust her vision to a more apostolic ministry for her sisters in the field of education in particular. This was because she saw that the strong contemporary pastoral need was paramount, over-riding other considerations. However, her community still retained a contemplative element in its Rule.

The issue did not go away because the founding of communities accelerated, with more and more emerging. The movement came from the parishes, where clergy and laity both felt enthused by the fruits of the Religious life. The pressure from the parochial level made it impossible for bishops to ignore or suppress the call to take vows. As the decades passed, more and more bishops began to receive vows and evolve pastoral and ecclesiastical processes to deal with problems that arose. The caveat they maintained was that there must be a path of release from the vows. As the 1885 Report to the upper house of Convocation (Canterbury) by the committee chaired by Harold Browne, Bishop of Winchester, expressed it:

> A vow, in the proper sense of the word, is a promise unreservedly made to God, which, therefore, if rightly and lawfully made, cannot be set aside – cannot be annulled by any authority but that of God Himself. But insomuch as cases have occurred, and do from time to time (however rarely) occur, in which the life-long engagement must be, or ought to be, set aside, a vow, as already defined, ought not to be taken. No engagement should therefore be made without the power of release to the Bishop. For the greater solemnity of the promise, and for the better understanding of his power of release, and its limits, the profession of a sister should be made to the Bishop himself.[2]

It was a subtle compromise. Religious could take vows to the bishop, but that in turn meant he could dispense them if required. Private vows made to God were vows he could not release anyone from. So the very demand of Religious that their vows should be received by a bishop and recognized by the Church was the very means by which the bishops now asserted their power of release! It was a neat and effective Anglican compromise.

The same standpoint of permitting the taking of Religious life vows while not regarding them as irrevocable can be seen too in the approach to male communities. The 1889 report, produced by a committee chaired by the Bishop of London, Frederick Temple, which considered the need for brotherhoods, advocated strongly that they should be formed. However, the committee both rejected and accepted vows as shown in the following contrasting extracts:

> The history of monastic and other institutions shows the dangers which arise from the assumption of irrevocable vows, taken, perhaps, at a period of exalted enthusiasm or intense depression, and afterwards unavailingly repented of ...

2 1885 Report to the Upper House of Convocation (Canterbury), *Chronicle of Convocation*, London: Rivingtons, p. 2.

> No Brotherhood of the kind contemplated could carry out efficient work without something analogous to the old vows of Poverty, Chastity and Obedience.[3]

For the Report's writers, the solution was to have temporary or dispensable vows that 'would often become life-long by the constant voluntary renewal of them'. This was eventually what the Lower House of the Canterbury Convocation accepted after much deliberation. The debate was peppered with some prejudiced comments from a few about vows being unscriptural, or 'not Anglican', or opening the Church of England to Jesuits and Rome! However, the arguments in favour carried the day.[4]

There were some who challenged the idea of having only dispensable vows. As Archdeacon Norris put it in the debate, when speaking of men who wished to take vows:

> These young men said that if they were to get up every morning knowing that it was an open question whether they continued in their special work or not, they dared not go on. There were dead points when they were discouraged, or not at their best, and they wished for vows to carry them over the dead points. In such cases if the vows were dispensable they would be subject to the temptation in times of discouragement to rush off to the superior and get a dispensation.[5]

However, this was a step too far for the church authorities in 1890. The passing of the resolutions did demonstrate that the story of the Religious vows among Anglicans was not a static standoff. There was a path from antipathy to tolerance to acceptance.

As the Victorian age moved on, the ground of the argument began to change. The 1897 Lambeth Conference showed that

3 1889 Report to the Upper House of Convocation (Canterbury), *Chronicle of Convocation*, London: Rivingtons, pp. 7–8.

4 Lower House of Convocation (Canterbury), 13 Feb 1890, *Chronicle of Convocation*, London: Rivingtons, p. 64.

5 Lower House of Convocation (Canterbury), 12 Feb 1890, *Chronicle of Convocation*, London: Rivingtons, p. 43.

bishops from different parts of the Communion as a whole were more accepting of the vows. Many now were content to encourage them and some defended them with conviction. A few evangelical bishops reiterated the old arguments, but theirs was a losing cause.[6] Bishop Charles Grafton, bishop of Fond du Lac in the USA, who had been for some years a member of the Society of St John the Evangelist (the influential men's community founded in 1866), spoke eloquently with respect to Religious life, which he insisted was a vocation and should be treated as such. Priesthood belonged to the corporate life of the Church, whereas a Religious vocation belonged 'to the economy of the Holy Ghost'. By this he meant that Religious communities needed to be free to develop as the Holy Spirit led them and not be hemmed in by too much regulation. This had an implication for the vows. Obedience to a Religious superior, for example, was a voluntary act of love, not the result of the legislative action of the Church. Unlike 'the fixity of ministerial orders', then, he believed the work of the Holy Ghost in the call of Religious life manifested itself in a variety of different forms. Bishops had to trust this call to have a corrective power in itself. With Religious, bishops were dealing with 'special devotional temperaments', he noted, that could be 'personally emotional'. He advocated bishops only concerning themselves with financial matters, property and good governance, not with matters such as vows.

However, the majority both in the debate and in the subsequent report and resolutions were firm that an avenue for dispensation of vows must be in every recognized community's constitution. This illustrated a shift away from opposing vows altogether, to one of how to regulate them. Nevertheless, despite these high-level discussions, no canons were implemented concerning the Religious life in the Church of England, nor were regulations codified about vows. This came partly because Bishop Edmund Knox[7] blocked the Province of York acting on the 1897 resolutions. The Archbishop of Canterbury

6 The 1897 Lambeth Conference debates at Lambeth Palace Library, LC38, pp. 129–86.

7 Bishop of Coventry 1894–1903, then of Manchester 1903–21.

therefore thought it pointless to proceed in the Province of Canterbury.

Among Religious themselves, however, a new struggle emerged. On one side were those who felt vows were now part of the Anglican ecclesiastical structure and they had to be viewed through an Anglican lens. The SSJE fathers, whose views dominated the papers sent to the 1897 Lambeth Conference and the subsequent reports, took this approach. The validity of vows would come from recognition given by the Anglican episcopate, especially the Archbishop of Canterbury, who could dispense them if required. Understanding and acceptance were the goals for these Religious, and by 1900 this had been largely achieved.

On the other side were the increasingly vocal Anglo-papalists, who were convinced that the driving force of the Catholic movement among Anglicans was corporate reunion with Roman Catholicism. The only path for Anglican Religious, therefore, was to adhere to Roman models and forms as much as possible. They embraced Roman Catholic canon law with respect to vows as well as liturgy and other matters. This became a major concern for Anglican bishops who saw this as a tussle over authority, not about the principle of vows. With little agreement between the sides, the end result was that there was no agreement among Religious themselves about the status of vows and so they were unable to support any form of regulation or canon law.

Ironically, this omission of action meant that Grafton's 'economy of the Holy Ghost' would be allowed to prevail. In the Church of England, instead of law came advice, dispensed by an Advisory Body (set up in 1935), meant to be temporary but which has evolved into permanence.[8] Suggestion, not compulsion, resulted in communities following its lead – an Anglican compromise accepted even by Anglo-papalists. This remained a viable path into the second half of the twentieth

8 The Advisory Council for Religious Communities in the Church of England (established in 1935) has more recently became a committee of the House of Bishops in 2018: see https://arlyb.org.uk/council-for-religious-communities (accessed 5 February 2022).

century, as Religious communities received fewer vocations; while Anglo-papalists became less vociferous after the Second Vatican Council, a Council that by embracing ecumenism and also radical change in the Religious life among Roman Catholics had undermined their original stance.

As the established communities became numerically reduced, the issue of their vows became uncontroversial. An established system for celibate Religious had been working without disagreement for many decades by the end of the twentieth century. In recent years, however, the issue of vows and their status has arisen again. Renewed interest in community life in the twenty-first century (as discussed in the Introduction to this book, and especially in the next chapter, Chapter 8) has seen the emergence of new groups and communities, some residential, others dispersed, some long-term, others temporary. The phenomenon has been loosely termed 'new monasticism,' but this is an umbrella term and in some cases can be misleading. Many of the communities do not claim to be 'monastic'. Most do not require celibacy.

The question has surfaced, perhaps inevitably, as to whether members of these new communities should consider the commitment of vows of some sort. As they evolve, the desire to find some sign of their members' relationship to one another and to God has become more pressing. Are vows the way to make a community sustainable in the long term? Are vows appropriate at all, and if so what sort of vows? How can the 'evangelical counsels' be interpreted for the current age – or should they not be simple promises instead?

Of the three vows of the 'evangelical counsels', poverty is less of a problem for new communities, as many have made arrangements to share resources. Nevertheless, dispersed communities where members are responsible for their own financial support can contain disparities of wealth and life-style, which may be an issue in some new communities. The response usually is to interpret poverty as 'simplicity' of life, with an expected generosity from members with whatever resources that are surplus to their basic needs. Especially in the 'Western' world, where societies are prone to over-consumption of resources, and in an age when ecological damage both to the earth and its climate are major challenges, a vow of poverty has a relevance and resonance to the contemporary generation.

Chastity is less easily translated into the new communities. When this vow means celibacy (no physical sexual relationships) it is not appropriate to communities where married members are permitted. Some groups have therefore interpreted the vow of chastity as meaning faithfulness to one's spouse if married, and celibacy only while single. However, fidelity to one's spouse is a significant element of the marriage vows and so, with this interpretation, a Religious vow of chastity would not be a fresh vow but a repetition or reaffirmation of something already promised; while for a single person to vow chastity only until (or if) they met someone they wished to marry, could not be a 'life-long' commitment.

The issue of chastity for new communities is accordingly complex. This is not to imply that this interpretation is 'inferior', or that it would be of less importance to the life of the church; but as the intention has been modified, there is a new distinction and it is not the same as a monastic vow. It might therefore be argued that this new interpretation of the vow of chastity can be made to the community, with temporary or life intention, but making it to the Church would pose further questions. For example, would such a revised vow still require a process of archepiscopal dispensation if the vocation did not hold?

And what of 'obedience'? Community obedience is not regarded now as akin to an army's chain of command, with an appointed ladder of ranks, but more as a shared sense of responsibility that is then put in the hands of an elected leader. It is about listening as much as giving orders. In a traditional monastic community the obedience is to the elected superior and/or the Chapter. But in new communities, leadership models can still be fluid. The settled will of the members as to how to elect a leader, and for how long, may not have been reached. It takes years before a new group is experienced enough to agree on a final constitution – far longer than is required to evolve a Rule of Life, this latter being about spiritual practice not administrative arrangements. The exercise of power and authority are matters that need trial and experimentation before a permanent structure can be fixed that suits the community's particular life and work. In any case, the dispersed model of community, common among the new groupings, makes leadership a difficult task. The onus of adherence to the Rule of the community is mostly on the individual member. It might be argued therefore that until a community is sufficiently evolved to have an agreed and transparent leadership, with mechanisms for regular elections, it is not possible to consider a vow of obedience.

The debates on these matters remain in their early stages. The challenge will be to retain flexibility about the role of Religious vows without diminishing their sacred intention. The vows of Religious can only be taken after a considerable period of testing in a novitiate. Then life vows are only possible after several years in simple vows. With new communities, this time of testing is even more significant, as the stability of the whole community may not have yet been firmly established. The problem here is that for some (though not all) members of new communities, rather than their acknowledgement by the Advisory Council being the symbol of acceptance by the Church, instead it has become the taking of vows endorsed by the Church.

Communities that are experimental and fragile can thus see the taking on of monastic terminology and the practice of vows as making them 'valid'. A community may adopt symbols and practices of a different type of Religious life in order to seek affirmation or recognition. Such desired recognition is not just that from the church authorities but from the Christian family as a whole. They are addressing their sense of newness and insecurity by looking to a long-established tradition and seeing themselves as a modern version of that. Such a view may be appropriate in general, but it also may not be in some cases – for that very action can affect the development and direction of a new community. It can stifle a new initiative as well as encourage it, for tradition can be a burden as well as a foundation.

The dangers may be avoided by a return to a simpler understanding of vows as a relationship with God (though of course with important public implications). The different types of vows and promises are a matter for the Church in distinguishing one type of Religious life from another. Yet all are in essence a response to God, a frail echo of the unbreakable promise and commitment of God to humanity. The purpose of any vow is not purely a personal piety but a desire to serve the people of God, whether in prayer or ministry. In this way, the relevance of the vows is also in the ongoing witness and service to which they lead. New communities may find it more helpful to concentrate on the *fruits* of whatever vows and promises they choose to take instead of being too anxious or anguished about their form and status.

Reflecting on the journey the Religious vows have taken through the last 175 years among Anglicans, there is a clear sense of caution at each stage, a caution that springs from the seriousness with which these vows should be taken. Recognition and understanding took decades rather than years. Private promises can be taken by anyone, but the Church has to wait to see communities thriving and viable before giving its public acknowledgement. This was frustrating for many of those who felt deeply about the meaning of their vows in former generations and who desired much quicker recognition. Yet, it is the patience of those early Religious and all they achieved that led to their eventual recognition. It was that witness that proved to the Church that the phenomenon of Religious life was of the Holy Spirit. The movement re-invigorated by Marian Hughes in 1841 is still evolving.

8

Journeying into New Monasticism

BEN EDSON

In this chapter Ben Edson provides insights into four quite different forms of 'new monasticism' which he has known in his own life. One, the evangelical Lee Abbey, eventually converted him to Christianity as a young student; a second, Moot, showed him how a novel contemporary 'monastic' life can galvanize into disciplined and transformative commitment those who are not even sure about their doctrinal beliefs; a third, the Church Army, has always had mission as its focus, but has renewed its vision of late in embracing the category of 'new monasticism'; and a fourth, Hopeweavers, has demonstrated the way in which a form of 'new monasticism' can collaborate with 'old monasticism' with spiritual benefits on both sides.

As a 16-year-old I moved to Lee Abbey, an ecumenical Christian community in North Devon. My father had been appointed as the Warden of Community, and so with my family I moved from London to rural Devon – at this point, my parents were Christians, but I was not. It was a slightly strange experience living as a non-Christian with a community of Christians. There is much that holds community life together at Lee Abbey, but most significant are the community 'promises' that each member of community makes when they join. Initially community members make their three 'initial membership' promises, and then after at least three months of living in community they decide whether to commit to 'full membership' and make a further seven promises.[1] Lee Abbey was established in 1946,

1 For the Lee Abbey 'promises', see the details at their website: https://leeabbeydevon.org.uk/community/promises/ (accessed 5 February 2022).

and the community that formed, which was centred on the Community Promises and a regular life of prayer, could now be described as an expression of 'new monasticism'. Living there was a formative time for me; at that time the majority of the people living in the community were westerners aged between 18–21 who were taking a gap year either before or after university. It was a melting pot where community members learnt more about themselves, one another, and their faith, in this pressure-cooker environment. I saw the good times and the bad times; I saw people arguing and people seeking reconciliation. The community simply accepted me; there were a few overzealous ones who tried to 'evangelize' me, but largely I was loved by the community.

There were many people who influenced me during my time at Lee Abbey – one was a man called John. Lee Abbey can be rather rarified: it is based on the North coast of Devon and is expensive for a family on an average income to attend, so that the community members tend to reflect this middle-class demographic. One afternoon I was in the courtyard of Lee Abbey and in the distance I could hear the sound of a motorbike; the sound got louder and then the motorbike pulled up to reception. A man dismounted the bike, removed his helmet, shed his leather jacket to reveal an armful of tattoos, and announced in a broad Yorkshire accent: 'I'm here to join the community.' He wasn't your typical community member but he proved to be an absolute gift to the community. He had a great sense of humour and people warmed to him quickly. He was open about his past, sharing with many that he had come to faith in prison through the ministry of a prison chaplain. John seemed to be settling in well to community life, but after about three months John locked himself in his room, drew his curtains and refused to speak with anyone. After 36 hours people were worried, and so one of the chaplains decided to access the room to make sure John was okay. The window was open and the chaplain climbed in. John was curled up on the floor in the fetal position; he was weeping. He'd stolen the Communion wine and drunk it, and he was deeply ashamed. He was hugged and held tight, and as he wept he said: 'I've never been loved like this before.' The love of a community can indeed be transformative for many people, and John's experience of being loved by community was by no means unique to him. At its best the Lee Abbey community was the most loving family a person could experience, held together through the community promises and a shared corporate rhythm of prayer. Lifelong friendships were formed at Lee Abbey as people lived in community and shared the highs and lows of life.

Lee Abbey was founded by Roger De Pemberton just after World War II as a residential community of people to run a conference centre dedicated to the renewal of the Church. The early vision was for an evangelistic centre where residential house parties were the primary method of evangelism. One of the founding fathers was the Revd Jack Winslow, the first chaplain of Lee Abbey, who lived there from 1948–62. His influence was formative in the shaping of the community life. Winslow had spent from 1914–34 in India, where he had established *Christa Seva Sangh*, a Christian ashram established to heal inter-racial strife. The Christian ashram movement sought to combine the Christian faith with the Hindu ashram model, and Christian monasticism with the Hindu Sannyasa tradition. The purpose of *Christa Seva Sangh* was to provide a small fellowship where Indians and Europeans could live together as Indians. Half the year was spent in study and training at the central ashram, and the other half in touring for evangelistic work. In these Christian ashrams we can start to see some of the values of Lee Abbey: 'monasticism', evangelism and dialogue. Indians and westerners were living alongside one another and learning from one another, and this breadth was replicated in the ecumenical nature of the burgeoning Lee Abbey community. The idea that Lee Abbey, with its mixed group of laypeople, could actually *be* a community was initially hard to grasp. One church dignitary is reputed to have commented that he didn't approve of monks and nuns living together. But as you could read on an early version of the website:

> Lee Abbey seeks to serve the whole Church, from a non-denominational standpoint. Members of the community come from a wide span of denominations, from Roman Catholic to Brethren, and in the same way it is hoped that all

> the guests who come to stay will feel as equally welcomed and at home whatever their Church tradition.

And so it was that, 50 years after it was founded, I found myself living in the community at Lee Abbey, and building friendships. After a few years I went away to university and within my first few weeks found myself at the centre of a quite hedonistic group of friends. We were living within a few streets of each other, and were in and out of one another's houses: we'd share meals, share drinks and we'd party together – a community of people enjoying life. The year ended and I hitched to the Glastonbury festival where I spent the final ten days of my first year of university before slowly making my way home. Once again I was quickly incorporated into the community: I'd build friendships again with the community members, and they would simply accept me for who I was. Gradually over the months and years, however, I started to note that the contrast between these two communities of people with whom I mixed was very marked: one was pleasure-oriented and self-centred, and the other – while flawed in many ways – was seeking to live with Christian values guiding them. I began to understand what drove the Lee Abbey folk, what shaped them; and it was through the day-to-day witness of the community that I discovered the Christian faith for myself.

Thus I had originally joined the community (brought there by my family) as a person who would *not* self-identify as Christian; and yet after journeying with the community over several years, this had changed. It was not one person but rather the witness of the whole community that spoke into my being. And it wasn't that community life was a 'utopian' experience; rather it was how the community sought to love one another and reconcile to one another after conflict – and believe me, there was conflict! Community is hard: community is brokenness and vulnerability; it is warts and all. The first of the further seven community promises is: 'Are you prepared to learn to live in fellowship, being open to be known for who you are, accepting one another in love, and saying of others nothing that could not be said to them personally if love and wisdom required it?' This was the promise that community members seemed to wrestle with taking the most, but it was the vital promise of honesty in community. Lee Abbey provided me with rooted experience in a community committed to love, reconciliation, and honesty, despite the pain that could cause. This pointed me more deeply to the relational love of a trinitarian God who – I came to believe – gave energy and meaning to the love expressed by community. I remain convinced that mission is an expression of the love of this God of community.

Community shapes people profoundly, and for a significant number of people the time that they had at Lee Abbey was a time where they sought to discern their vocation. For some that was a vocation to ordained ministry; for two or three, a vocation to the Religious life; but for all, a calling back to the demands of baptismal vows. The three community promises that every member of community makes as they join the community give a framework for this ongoing baptismal vocation:

> *Promise 1*: Do you affirm before the Community your personal faith in Christ and your desire through prayer, study and service to seek a deep and mature faith? **I do.**
> *Promise 2*: Do you understand by this that your mind, your time, your talents, your possessions and all your relationships are to be increasingly surrendered to Christ as Lord? **I do.**
> *Promise 3*: Do you promise to be loyal to the Community in its aims, its work, its standards of behaviour, and its disciplines? **I do.**

The promises, the community, the evangelistic focus, and an experience of a new form of 'monasticism', are formative for the individuals who join the community, who in turn then serve the wider Church. The Hussite and Moravian reformers had a phrase, '*Ecclesiola in Ecclesia*', meaning 'little Church in the Church,' or 'little churches within a church'. The people who believed in the idea of the '*ecclesiola*' were not out to change the whole Church all at once, but to form a Church within a Church which would form a nucleus of true believers inside the general Church. Their object in the formation of this nucleus was that it might act as a leaven and influence the life of the whole Church for the better. Perhaps this is what Lee Abbey is: a nucleus of people who are formed by a return to their baptismal vows and who then become the leaven in the wider Church. Is this then, more generally, the calling of the wider 'new monastic' movement?

Through Lee Abbey, new monasticism has had a significant influence on the direction of my life, and so it is within that personal background that I continue through this chapter. I will explore three further communities here, and through their narratives journey into some of the opportunities and challenges that they face and which are emblematic of those that the wider movement confronts. (These communities correlate with the three distinct types of new monastic life identified by Ian Mobsby, Chris Neal and Colin, CSWG (Community of the Servants of the Will of God) in a briefing paper presented to the *Advisory Council for Religious Life* in 2012.)

On this basis the first type that I will explore is the 'networked new monastic communities'. These are intentional missional networks of at least two localized communities with a shared rhythm of life. The aforementioned briefing paper of 2012 states: 'The Moot Community aspires to grow in this way although it only has one localised community at the moment'. It is the Moot community – as I first encountered it – that I have chosen to represent this first type. In its first incarnation Moot described itself as: 'a new monastic community that seeks to live in a way that is honest to God and honest to now'.[2]

The second type of new monastic community is 'mission order communities'. The core purpose of these communities is Christian mission. These missional new monastic communities focus their energies on mission and evangelism in places where the wider Church presence is weak. Here the communities and rhythms of life primarily serve the apostolic mission endeavour. The mission community that I explore here is the Church Army: a mission community open to all Christians who have a passion for evangelism and whose vision is 'for everyone everywhere to encounter God's love, and be empowered to transform their communities through faith shared in words and action.'[3]

---

2 The website of the present community is: https://www.mootcommunity.org/ (accessed 5 February 2022).

3 https://churcharmy.org/who-we-are/our-mission/ (accessed 5 February 2022).

The final and third type of new monastics are 'localised intentional communities', or particular small local expressions with a shared rhythm of life – although many have, or plan to have, some form of motherhouse. The community that I have chosen to represent this type of new monasticism is The Community of Hopeweavers, which describes itself as 'a dispersed fellowship of friends who seek God together through stillness, silence and creativity, sharing the ups and downs of life wherever we are called to live and work.'[4]

As I peruse blogs, books and websites, I read of a diverse new monastic movement that is visibly changing the world in some significant ways. I read of young Christians committing themselves to a radical life of discipleship, and I'm excited and encouraged by what I read. However, in honesty I also experience a level of scepticism as I ask: Is this really true? Is there a rebirth in monasticism occurring in the West, and if so is it really going to serve to renew the Church, or is it all a manifestation of personal hubris? Will it come and go, given that the roots are only as yet in shallow soil?

I write this as a friend of the new monastic movement, for as I've already disclosed, one early expression of new monasticism influenced my life in a profound way. At the same time, I have some theological reservations and linguistic concerns around the misappropriation of the language of 'monasticism' surrounding the movement. Of course, language evolves and on one level a change in the use and understanding of the language of 'new monasticism' is a small matter. However, one could also argue that the lack of clarity or common understanding exposed by poorly used language highlights a fault-line in emerging expressions of new monasticism. This is moreover a fault line that, if deepened, has the potential to cause fracture in what, overall, I believe to be a movement of the Spirit in our times.

The language we use about this movement is significant – maybe particularly so around self-identification. In my research for this chapter it quickly became clear that many new groups actually wanted to resist the 'new monastic' label, and

4 https://hopeweavers.org.uk/about-us/ (accessed 5 February 2022).

I also noted this same resistance at a recent conference of those involved in new monasticism. However, despite the limitations of language, I appeal for a generosity of spirit from those who have been irritated by the term as I use it within this chapter. Alongside that, I appeal for wisdom and respect from those involved in the new monastic movement. As I first began to work on this chapter, Leicester Diocese had started advertising for a prior of a new monastic community (The Community of the Tree of Life), with the BBC reporting that 'Leicester monastery ad wants prior with social media skills'.[5] I can fully understand the irritation that many who have dedicated their life to (old) monasticism feel at the misappropriation of such language, and therefore appeal to those involved in new monasticism to listen more closely to the traditions from which they draw. It may well be that a new language is required and will evolve; but in this period of emergence and transition I will retain the 'new monastic' terminology in order to reflect on the contribution that the movement is making to Church and mission, using phraseology which I hope does not alienate but instead denotes shared understandings and meaning.

Moot

Twenty or so years ago I, alongside a number of other people from the USA, Australia and the UK, was invited to a consultation at Fuller Theological Seminary on 'The Emerging Church'. I travelled over and shared a room with a person whom I'd met once or twice before: his name was Ian Mobsby. Ian was in the process of establishing an emerging church called Moot and I was in the process of establishing an emerging church called Sanctus1. We shared stories and experiences, and reflected on what we'd learnt on our shared but distinct journeys. At that point Moot was based at St Matthew's, Westminster, and Ian was serving his curacy there, while Santcus1 was based at Manchester Cathedral and I was a Church Army officer. Ian

5 http://www.bbc.co.uk/news/uk-england-leicestershire-38665859 (accessed 5 February 2022).

became a good friend and we shared stories and met regularly at various events and conferences.

After a number of years both Sanctus1 and Moot had grown. We had both featured in the *Mission Shaped Church* report, and people were keen to hear us tell our stories and to reflect on practice. At Sanctus1 we started to reflect on its identity, and as part of that process we began to discern our 'values'. A small group met, and four values were identified which were held under the umbrella value of 'covenanted'. The intention was that we would seek to transition to a community that was held together through covenanted relationships with one another. Once a year we would make promises to the wider Church and to one another to commit radically and sacrificially to Sanctus1 and our mission to city-centre Manchester. I was excited by the possibility and presented the vision to the community. I got much wrong in my presentation and the language used was not quite right; and the people who were part of Sanctus1 at that time said no to the concept of a covenanted relationship. They didn't like the word, it seems because they liked their loose connections to one another and wanted to know why more was being asked of them. And after much dialogue another group formed and reflected further, and the word and ethos of 'covenanted' was disposed of, and the four other values adopted without any overarching framework. As I've thought further about this over the years I know that we lost something radical and countercultural at this point. We were poised to take a bold step into something new: we were about to step into the 'new monastic' realm without us even knowing it or having the language to understand it; but it was uncomfortable for people, and it became clear that this bold step is not one that everyone can make.

Ian and I had continued talking, and he started to share with me the direction that he thought that Moot was taking. Ian had been influenced by a mutual friend, the Revd Karen Ward, at The Church of the Apostles in Seattle, and their own experiment with new monasticism. Karen was their Abbess, and a community of people with her were outworking their faith through community vows and a rhythm of prayer. Moot grew and evolved, too, moving from St Matthew's, Westminster to

St Mary's, Aldermary – one of the oldest churches in the city of London. Sanctus1 had in the meantime formed a partnership with the Methodist Church and we'd establish *Nexus* – an arts café in the city centre of Manchester – and Ian had been working with the Diocese to establish *Host* – a café at the back of St Mary's. They had also started *Stressed Out in the City*: a meditation group for city workers that was regularly attracting 50 people, and based on the teaching of John Main, OSB with regular Taizé worship. We shared stories between us, but the significant difference was that Moot was now being steered firmly down the 'new monastic' route, and as I met with members of the community they were excited about the radical step that they were taking. Moot was developing what it called a 'rhythm of life', with various practices and postures being adopted; and clearly this was a moment of greater self-definition and disciplined commitment. As they then affirmed:

> At the heart of a rhythm of life is the desire to know and follow the way of Christ wherever you are. For us, that's the busy city of London, with all its many and varied challenges. For example, it is easy to see spirituality as just one part of life – as a Sunday affair. The rhythm of life, however, helps us to see God in every moment, to hear the voice of the Spirit calling us to join with whatever God is doing, wherever that might be. In that sense, it is also a call to mission, to bringing good news to broken and fragmented lives (Moot, 'Introduction to a Rhythm of Life').

My time at Sanctus1 drew to a close after about seven years, and I gather that the transition was hard for the community. I have already explained the circumstances. Yet after about five more years Ian's time also came to a close at Moot, and I gather that this too was a hard transition for Moot. However, I was aware of all the positive things that had then happened through Moot. For instance, I knew of a number of people who had been selected for ordination and for whom Moot was foundational; moreover, their worship was an inspiration, and the wider new monastic movement was growing in influence as a result. Moot was thus celebrated as a prime exemplar of new monasticism, featured in countless books, promoted on websites, and often featured at conferences on new monasticism. In many ways it was therefore possible at the time to regard them as the 'go-to' community in this movement.

It was during this time of transition, then, that I interviewed the new chaplain to the Moot community, the Revd Andrew Norwood. Norwood was an interim appointment whom the Diocese asked to journey with Moot after Ian left, and many of the founding community had transitioned out. The remnant at that time was a group of 20 or so people meeting on a Sunday, and reflecting anew on their identity; Andrew Norwood was facilitating the community in this process. He told me:

> The 'new monastic' thing has now been put on the backburner as a more contemplative expression of community forms. Much initial energy was expended on it, but the group now needs to sustain a Guild Church, manage a café, and organise themselves as a community; and at this point in their life they are doing well simply to survive. The 'rhythm of life' that had been developed had little impact on the community at large, with many starting to read the provisions for it, but giving up on the second or third page as it didn't resonate with their life experience.

From this it was clear that the community was then in a time of transition, and with much stripped away from the earlier ('monastic') vision the community was reforming itself once more. They were a vulnerable but faithful community, and yet in this new time of transition much could be seen that previously was hidden. Perhaps what was being exposed was a fragile underside of the new monasticism: that is, once a founding community has moved on, there may be little that is left. A short-term commitment creates a short-term community, whereas a life vow creates (at least potentially) a community of stability. In other words, an initial charism is located in a community at a particular moment, and with a charismatic leader the charism can be located *in* that person. The charismatic person is then both the gatekeeper and the story-teller, the priest and the publicist, and this is a mix that has much power and authority – but also has a potential toxicity. In contrast, the choosing of an Abbot in the Rule of St Benedict follows the guiding principle that the man 'be the one selected either by the whole community acting unanimously in the fear of God, or by some part of the community, no matter how small, which possesses sounder judgment'. In this alternative, and more ancient, vision, then, an Abbot is elected from *within* a community: he is not either appointed externally, or self-appointed (though it is worth noting that a founding Abbot may, in unusual circumstances, establish a community *de novo*). Once elected, however, a Benedictine Abbot is called to 'recognize that his goal must be profit for the monks, not pre-eminence for himself' (*Rule of St Benedict*, Chapter 64: 'The Election of an Abbot', 8). In a media-saturated world, where self-promotion is all too easy, this is an important corrective from the Rule of St Benedict, and draws attention to the implicit dangers of a 'new monasticism' that establishes its own rules as it goes along.

My own hope for Moot, then a community that I was personally very fond of, was that in the stripping away of its original form it would still be the liturgy of the community that served to sustain it. But at least in its moment of transition that I have been describing here, this was not obviously the case. There was no rhythm of prayer, no corporate prayer, and the new chaplain was having to work hard to establish a way of being that was life-giving to the community. The 'new monastic' label had been a weight that had been owned by a previous community, but was not obviously one that this new community was then willing to shoulder. The danger was that it might not be life-giving after all, but even life-sapping: it was an open question.[6]

Moot was thus situated in a transient context, and ministered to a transient people-group: it appears that this was part of its charism. And thus here we see a contrast with the traditional

6 I have not followed closely the later developments of the community but I note that the website now affirms that 'as a community, we share a Rhythm of Life. This defines our core values and guides what we do. With the Rhythm at our centre, others can join with us, to be and to belong.' https://www.mootcommunity.org/ (accessed 5 February 2022).

Religious communities. They are by nature firmly located in *place*, with a 'Rule of Life' bigger than any individual or even any one particular community. In contrast, Moot has moved on over the years, and even when it appeared to have settled in a place the charism of the community was not obviously planted deeply enough to sustain change. My question at the time was: is it like the seed that grew in the rocky soil that did not have roots strong enough, and so flourished for a time and then faded? Happily it continues to grow in new ways.

There is a lesson within the early history of Moot with regards to sustainability and transience. Moot sought to speak into a culture of transience, and yet at that point it was the transience within the community itself that served at times to destabilize it. In contrast, the traditional Religious life provides an obvious answer to this problem – a stable base in the storm. Yet at the same time it is also conceivable that the answer that it provides is not the answer to the question being asked today. It is so counter-cultural now, that it might be a step too far for a community that also prides itself on being engaged with contemporary culture. The call to the Religious life is a significant call, a call that is tested by the community, the Church and the individual. It is a call that involves a journeying towards a destination rather than a sudden arrival at one. In this sense, the witness of networked new monastic communities leaves us with a continuing set of alluring questions.

The contrast with our second example of new monasticism may therefore be instructive.

Church Army

In 1996 I started to explore my own vocation seriously. I had a strong sense of call to mission, and to the Anglican Church, but was certain at that time that I was not being called to ordination as such. I spoke with a few people and started to wonder whether I was being drawn to offer myself for selection as a Church Army officer. I was unsure whether the name, the uniforms and the old-fashioned militaristic nature of the organization put me off; but I met with people there and was inspired by the work that they were doing, and so eventually put myself forward for selection. I was selected, and started to train at the Church Army College in Sheffield. It was a structured experience with lectures, tutor groups, morning prayer and a twice-weekly Eucharist, and as I learnt more of the history of Church Army I started to understand the organisation more. Towards the end of my time at training college we had a number of sessions exploring Church Army's history, and at these sessions we were introduced to the Church Army Rule of Life. Church Army's founder, Wilson Carlile, established the organisation in 1882 with three principles: 'conversion', 'consecration' and 'Christian community', and it was on these three 'C's' that the Rule of Life was based. 'Consecration', in particular, spoke of a life that was set aside for God and that was structured by the Rule of Life. However, I have to confess that, at that point in our training, my fellow students and I knew very little about the Rule of Life. At our commissioning service we adopted it formally, but – personally speaking – it had very little direct impact on my life and ministry at the time. It was certainly not a Rule that I had reflected on deeply, and thus I cannot say that it 'shaped' me at this stage in my formation.

But in 2012 the Church Army transitioned into being an Acknowledged Mission Community as it sought to reshape its identity and the way that people engaged with Church Army. Part of this reform was a re-engagement with its Rule of Life. And this is way we can now say that a second type of new monastic community is the Mission Order Communities, with their core theological purpose of Christian mission. In 2012 I attended the launch service of the Church Army Mission Community at St Paul's Cathedral; and five years later I spoke with Captain Andrew Chadwick CA – the Dean of Community for the Church Army – who told me:

> Church Army does not *formally* associate with the new monastic movement, but it is a community that has a Rule of Life to which over 500 people have subscribed, and it is dispersed nationally, from Aberdeen to Guernsey and from West Wales to East Anglia. Church Army is however still in a time of transition. The Mission Community was only launched

> five years ago and they are bedding down and learning what their new identity means. The earlier form of the community had 'defined itself to death'; this gave them no space to grow and now they are seeking simply to inhabit the space that they are in, rather than define or constrain themselves any further.

There are, therefore, now five different pathways of belonging within Church Army, with different levels of commitment on each pathway. For example, a 'commissioned member' will be committed to the Rule of Life, pray for Church Army and regularly attend the regional cluster meetings; whereas people on the 'companion pathway' simply want to show their support for the work of Church Army. Chadwick commented:

> Church Army is largely made up of activists, people who are fed by doing their work; so the challenge is for their doing to come from their being. As Dean of Community I am seeking to facilitate that, to slow the activist down, to provide support, reduce isolation and ensure that the appropriate spiritual structures are in place for them to flourish and succeed.

Anyone who has spent time with a monastic community will know that part of the way that the community 'slows down' is through a regular rhythm of prayer. Prayer will be said at various points through the day. It punctuates everything and gives rhythm to the community. An important area of learning from the traditional monastic life for the new monastic, particularly the mission-focused communities, concerns the relationship between prayer and mission. A number of years ago I was in a seminar on prayer that was led by a wise nun in her 80s. I looked at her and thought to myself, 'You are a deeply religious and prayerful woman, and I can learn much from you'; and then she started her seminar by saying, 'After 40 years of a life of prayer I am only just learning how to pray!' Such people who have been committed to a whole life of prayer are still *learning* about prayer; and the new monastic movement has much in turn to learn from them about mission and prayer. There is of course significant history concerning traditional monasticism and the relationship between mission and prayer. The sixth-century Irish missionary monks who left Ireland and shared their new-found faith with the neighbouring islands were people rooted in prayer, Columba being perhaps the most famous of these who founded the Abbey on the island of Iona. Columbanus also ventured into Europe and founded three monasteries in France which became centres of training and evangelism; from there many other centres in that region were established. Through Columbanus's 'peregrination' (*peregrination pro Christo*) a large part of Europe was introduced to Christianity and to monasticism, and prayer and mission sat alongside one another in these important developments.

Inspired by examples such as these I had, in a previous incumbency, established a small community called 'Abide'. Abide was a new monastic community that sought to follow five 'rhythms of grace': each year the community would gather and commit to living by these rhythms of grace. The five rhythms of grace (adopted from the Community of St Chad in Lichfield Diocese) sought to find a healthy balance between prayer and mission. As we adopted the rhythms of grace a number of people said to me: 'Ben, as a Church isn't this what we're meant to be doing anyway?' I'd reply, 'Yes it is, but it can be helpful to adopt these to give focus to our vocational call as baptized people.' In Abide we sought to put prayer and mission together as flip sides of the same coin.

There are two movements within the Trinity that are 'rhythmically' related to one another: adoration and procession. Love is given and love is returned. So, the Son is the perfect image of the Father, adoring the Father as he is adored, and the Son is also the one sent into the world. The Word made flesh retires to the mountain to pray and comes down the mountain to love and serve the world. The Church participates in this rhythm: there is the gathering of Christians as the Church, and the mission or sending out of the Church to be Christians in the world. This rhythm correlates with prayer and mission. The Christian community 'gathered' in is a community that is called to worship, and much of worship is of course prayer; and then that community is sent out to proclaim the gospel externally. The invitation that I believe that both traditional Religious communities and new monastic communities have accepted is to reflect this dimension of the triune God's 'exit' and 'return', being both eternally sent and eternally in personal communion. One of the significant contributions of new monasticism to the Church is thus the naming and reclaiming of mission as part of the monastic heritage. This is what Church Army is seeking to outwork, and this has parallels with other mission organisations that have also sought to learn and be shaped by the Religious life. The Church Mission Society (CMS) has also transitioned into becoming an Acknowledged Mission Community; and The Order of Mission (TOM), birthed from St Thomas Crookes in Sheffield, leads a life of simplicity, purity and accountability, as a contemporary re-interpretation of the monastic vows of poverty, chastity and obedience. Thus three communities whose primary charism is one of mission have sought to learn afresh from the traditional Religious life. The challenge, which Chadwick identified above, is to keep the two movements of prayer and mission rhythmically related to one another. In an activist community such as Church Army prayer could very easily become a secondary movement, and this would be a disservice to the monastic heritage that it is drawing from.

The life of the Church needs both prayer and mission, two movements that are rhythmically related to one another, just as breathing requires us both to breathe in and breathe out in order to sustain bodily life. This is what the new monastic movement is seeking to do, but this is a challenge to a strongly activist movement. There is much wisdom within the traditional Religious communities and an openness and willingness to share this wisdom.

And as we shall now see, a similar lesson can be drawn from my third, and final, example of new monasticism.

The Community of Hopeweavers

The Community of Hopeweavers is based in Southampton. Their Guardian is Jacqui Lea, and as I spoke with her a few years ago, I thought to myself, 'Hopeweavers: what an apt name'. In fact they do not actually self-describe as a new monastic community, preferring instead the term 'Acknowledged Anglican Religious Community', which of course seems not quite as 'marketable' as 'new monasticism' but serves to locate their own community within a process of discernment and recognition by the wider Church.

The Community of Hopeweavers first came into being in 2007, and by 2015 had been through the process of acknowledgment and become recognized by the wider Church. Their website[7] says that their purpose is:

> To advance the Christian Faith for the public benefit, in accordance with the doctrines of the Church of England mainly but not exclusively by:
> Providing sanctuary and creative space using Christian based resources for individuals, families and groups, of any faith or none, to engage in the ancient practice of stillness and silence.
> Providing a dispersed community, united through a common rhythm of life, which Christians from any denominations can join, should they want to include contemplative, monastic Christian practices as part of their Christian faith.

Already in 2015 Hopeweavers were formally 'acknowledged', and by the end of 2016 they had 38 Members plus ten enquirers, living according to a Rule of Life and renewing annual 'promises' in front of their Episcopal Visitor at the start of Advent. Jacqui told me:

> We are ecumenical and very mixed and come from a growing area – folks from local diocesan areas including Winchester, Portsmouth, Salisbury, Oxford and Guildford: a mix of lay and ordained people. Over 20 different churches and traditions are represented in this group – people from all denominations with about a third from outside the Anglican tradition – mostly from Vineyard, Baptist and independent churches. People comment on the joy of having a simple daily office and Rule that act as a focus for us as disciples of Jesus, regardless of our starting points.

7 https://hopeweavers.org.uk/ (accessed 5 February 2022).

Each member is also part of a Community of Hopeweavers small group, that will meet about six to eight times a year to encourage and share the journey of living to a Rule of Life. These groups are seen as additional to local church membership. Both 'members' and 'enquirers' are also invited to be part of Cloister Days – times and spaces set aside for the community to gather together. They participate and lead weekly times of prayer and Friday midday Holy Communion, alongside other forms of prayer and practical service.

The relationship of Hopeweavers with the various other local Religious communities has been significant, and was helped by the process of 'acknowledgement'. There was a two-way learning within this transition. The route to acknowledgment required the new community to be in relationship with an established Religious community. For Hopeweavers the initial relationship was with the Anglican Franciscans at Hilfield Friary. At the beginning there was a process of getting to know one another, but once the relationship was established it was a relationship of mutual flourishing. Quiet days and retreats are regularly held at the Friary as they journey alongside the Franciscan community. Alongside Hilfield Friary there are significant friendship with a number of other traditional monastic communities and new monastic communities too. As Jacqui reported:

> The traditional Religious communities who particularly support us and our developing charism in addition to Hilfield Friary, are The Sisters of the Love of God at Fairacres (SLG) in Oxford, the Community of St Mary the Virgin in Wantage (CSMV), The Community of the Servants of the Will of God at Crawley Down (CSWG), and our nearest location-wise – the Sisters of Bethany in Southsea (SSB). The Northumbria Community[8] has also been a significant friend.

There is a difference in vocation between the new and the old, but a mutual respect has been built through a valuing of the different and yet complementary communities. Also, as

8 See https://www.northumbriacommunity.org/ (accessed 5 February 2022), which is another 'dispersed' modern movement providing a 'new way of living'.

already mentioned, Hopeweavers has never explicitly used the language of 'new monasticism' of itself, and I have no doubt that this has been a positive factor in the flourishing of the relationship with the established Religious communities, since they can often harbour some scepticism or suspicion about the idea of creating 'monasticism' afresh.

Some Concluding Reflections

The relationship between the established and the emerging forms of 'monasticism' is one that begs further theological reflection at the conclusion of this narrative. As long ago as 1974 Ralph Winter wrote a paper with the catchy title, 'The Two Structures of God's Redemptive Mission'.[9] In it Winter identified two structures of Church that have historically been at work in the mission of God – he calls these structures 'the modal' and 'the sodal'. In recent years missiologists have taken hold of these categories with some vigour. The 'modal', based on the word 'mode', represents the customary way in which things are done – with regards to a church structure, this is the settled parish church. A church of this sort is located in a central, public place where all who want to are welcome to belong: it has low 'boundaries' and is an inclusive safe place for all. The 'sodal', in contrast, based on the Latin *sodalis* (meaning companion, comrade, friend) is an altogether different structure, much closer to a fraternity with a set of rules for those who join it – if you like, a monastic community. Winter argues that these two structures are needed within the Church, the modal for its low boundaries and inclusion, and the sodal for its focus and intentionality. However, both are problematic on their own – the modal can become inward-looking and maintenance-focused, and the sodal can feel superior and exclusive. I would like to suggest that new monasticism is an exploration of the space between the sodal and modal; for it is neither a modal community nor a sodal community, as

9 Winter, Ralph D., 1974, 'The Two Structures of God's Redemptive Mission', *Ecclesiology: An International Review*, 2, pp. 121–39.

such, but seeks to draw from both and hence can serve to bring renewal to both. The St Anselm community at Lambeth Palace walks this in-between place too – the renewal of the Religious life was one of the current Archbishop's priorities – but St Anselm's is not a monastic community in the traditional sense, but rather a short-term sodal-*like* community that lives in the space between the monastic life and the parish.[10]

Of the three groups we have explored here, the Hopeweavers appear to have embraced this in-between place with the greatest effect, for they are well respected and supported within their diocese and equally well respected by the local churches; and in addition to this they have excellent relationships with the nearby traditional Religious communities. There is no sense that they are an irritation to the Religious communities, however, and there is no sense either of 'sheep stealing' from the local churches. Rather they are a community that sits in this in-between place as it seeks to bring new life to both the local church and to the local Religious communities. This is a particular gift that the 'new monastic' can bring (albeit without even using the title!). I am thus convinced that a factor in the renewal of the Church will be these communities that continue to seek to inhabit this precious in-between space: they are short-term sodal communities in creative relationship with the modal.

In the same way, Abide members were also part of the parish church I described earlier, with Abide being just one of the expressions of belonging within the parish system. The majority of the people involved were originally part of a struggling evening congregation, but once Abide was established and embedded, the evening congregation started to grow in depth and in numbers – another instance of a sodal community within the modal. There were challenges that went with development, such as the danger of creating a two-tier membership where one group of people could be seen as more committed than another; but with grace and generosity these challenges were overcome. Abide served to bring renewal to the evening

---

10 For a more extended discussion of the St Anselm Community at Lambeth, see the 'Introduction', above.

congregation, which in turn served the wider church community through enquirers' courses and a night shelter for destitute asylum seekers. In many ways this is a returning to the '*Ecclesiola in Ecclesia*' model, re-thinking again the place of the necessary place of a leaven in the bread. And perhaps this highlights the most significant, and long-standing, feature of the call of 'new monasticism'.

As I have journeyed through the stories in this chapter I have reflected afresh on much which continues to bring me hope, but I also see once more how delicate and fragile a movement 'new monasticism' is. Over the years I've discovered that any personal hubris in leadership in these exploratory groups needs a firm and realistic stripping away; but under that there is a movement in the Spirit of people who are seeking authentically to reinterpret the Religious life for today. However, was we have also seen, this is not such a 'new' movement as we might imagine. Lee Abbey is 75 years old, Church Army is over 100 years old, the Northumbria Community is over 20 years old, and there are other communities alongside them that have been exploring this kind of creative path for many years. What has encouraged me most along the way in my own engagement and involvement with these groups is the dialogue between the traditional and the new, and the learning that there has been there when this has been authentically achieved. At the end of the day, then, the various flowerings of the contemporary 'new monastic' movement might well be seen as a call back to the fundamental vows of baptism: a call, in other words, to take our baptismal vows *seriously*, as life-changing, challenging, demanding, joyous and transformative unto death. And while such a message isn't anywhere near as marketable (sadly) in an established Church as the more alluring title of 'new monasticism', what the two propulsions have in common is a call to a deeper discipleship. And this is surely something greatly to be celebrated.

9

'Some Peculiar Genius': The 'Intentional Communities' of Little Gidding[1]

FRANCES WARD

In this chapter Frances Ward reflects on the first English revival of 'Religious life' after the Reformation at Little Gidding (under the extraordinary leadership of Nicholas Ferrar), and then on the later manifestations of community-living there in the twentieth century, inspired by Ferrar and energized afresh by T. S. Eliot's poetry. Ward echoes the lessons of the last chapter in drawing attention to the dangers of individual charism in shaping 'intentional communities' – how authoritarianism and abuse can creep into the mix when a community is not founded in a stable and moderate Rule such as that of St Benedict, in which power is carefully dispersed. Yet Little Gidding has maintained its allure over the centuries, and still symbolizes the importance of attention to place, time, nationality and stability in forging lasting communities of witness to Christ.

1 In this chapter, the term 'intentional community' is used to apply to those who are drawn together with a particular vision of communal life that is generated by that community itself. Often led by a charismatic or authoritative leader, such communities will tend to draw on that person's religious or spiritual inspiration. They are to be distinguished from 'Religious communities' as such (many of which, of course, also began with an inspirational founder such as St Benedict, St Dominic, or St Francis), which have continued through time with a sustained, living tradition that transcends any one individual or particular group.

'If you came this way'

The pilgrim to Little Gidding[2] today slips easily back to May 1936 when T. S. Eliot found his way along the rough road between hedgerows of voluptuary sweetness, to the dull façade of the small church. He wrote the fourth of his *Four Quartets* later, in 1941,[3] as he watched for fires from London roofs, contemplating the meaning of 'England', for which so many were dying. He wondered aloud in the poem about the ruptures he saw, as he distilled the modernist and anticipated the postmodernist condition, seeing only 'a shell, a husk of meaning'. He wrote of memory and desire, of forgetting and remembering, of the timelessness and place that spoke of eternity, of pattern and form, as he recalled the time he imagined England at Little Gidding:

> Here, the intersection of the timeless moment
> Is England and nowhere. Never and always.

Today, pilgrims will often sit in the church at Little Gidding and recite the words of the poem, consciously seeking to experience something tangible in this place 'where prayer has been valid' – an engagement with roots of Anglican spirituality that extend back to the early years of the seventeenth century. With varying degrees of questioning and self-consciousness, they look for a sense of authenticity, to re-inhabit a tradition and a world that was already disappearing as Eliot wrote.

Inspiring a peculiar mix of nostalgia and utopianism, Little Gidding is a place that appeals to a small cross-section of today's Britain. You are unlikely to see millennials making their way there, or much diversity of faith or culture represented in visitors. Little Gidding offers a quintessentially 'traditional' English vision and spirituality that is at odds with much British contemporary culture. As such, it raises questions of how diverse

---

2 Little Gidding is a small village approximately nine miles North-West of Huntingdon in Cambridgeshire, right at the edge of the boundary of the Anglican diocese of Ely.

3 Eliot, T. S., 1942, *Four Quartets*, London: Faber and Faber. Extracts from 'Little Gidding' are used by permission.

British national identities relate to this cul-de-sac within the Anglican traditions of the Church of England. There are other questions too: of what happens to the shadows and nightmares that post-colonial Britain cannot deny; of the importance of time and place to the present mobile lifestyles that are transient and accelerating, often self-absorbed and intentionally of the moment. In a United Kingdom that voted for Brexit in 2016, laying wide open divisions and fierce contestation on 'united' national identity and what 'Englishness' signifies, such questions are raw and urgent. What does it mean today to 'vow to thee, my country'?[4] There seems, more than ever, a need to capture the imagination of the nation, to provide a sense of belonging in time and place, to draw disparate peoples together into a common vision and sense of nationality that is not tribal and introspective, defensive or xenophobic. Can such places, like Little Gidding, and other pilgrim destinations like Walsingham, Lindisfarne, or Iona, offer anything at all, apart from a retreat from a confusing world? Or does pilgrimage contribute to those debates about national identity? Is it the case that, as Andrew Rumsey reflects, 'it is vital that the Church reckons with its English calling, not least so that the idea of England may be reclaimed for all who live there and that fruitful relations may be grown with neighbours who do not'?[5] Perhaps the history and traditions of Little Gidding, with the 'peculiar genius' of the place born of long experience of living with conflicts and shadows, have lessons that are worth attention. Rumsey's book on the parish offers fruitful reflection on the significance of place in the creation of meaning through time, giving a sacramental understanding that enables fresh insight into the importance of pilgrimage sites such as Little Gidding.

The story of Little Gidding from the seventeenth century onwards is also the story of lay communities seeking to witness to Jesus Christ in their daily lives. With psychological depth of insight, Iris Murdoch explored some of the dangers that can

4 'I Vow to Thee, My Country' is a British patriotic hymn, created in 1921, when a poem by Sir Cecil Spring Rice was set to music by Gustav Holst. Some people now refuse to sing it; while others are moved deeply.

5 Rumsey, Andrew, 2017, *The Parish: An Anglican Theology of Place*, London: SCM Press, p. 6.

perplex and destroy such experiments in communal living in her novel *The Bell* – as astute today as it was when published in 1958.[6] Perhaps we see the end of an era, when lessons have been learned from such experiments. The lay person, seeking to belong to a particular place, or community, is now more likely, if Anglican, to join the Franciscan Third Order or to become a Benedictine 'oblate', following a personal Rule alongside a group or belonging to a Benedictine convent or monastery. Taking vows as an oblate Benedictine, for instance, entails a postulancy and novitiate of two years, and living a Rule that includes daily prayer, biblical reading in the particular Benedictine way of *Lectio Divina*,[7] Holy Communion at least once a week, an annual retreat and spiritual direction. It calls for active sympathy with the Benedictine values of conversion of life, stability and continuity, obedience, humility and hospitality, following the spirit of the early sixth-century Rule of St Benedict. They are taken in all seriousness, as a public vow before the community of monks or nuns, and are understood to be life-long. Without the anchor of the monastic community, intentional communities can prove to be less resilient. As a key character in Murdoch's *The Bell*, Catherine, comments: 'It's difficult, you know, for a lay community where nothing's ordained. It all has to be invented as you go along.'[8] It is not many intentional communities that make the transition to an on-going institutional life that transcends the personality of the founder. Perhaps the community founded at Taizé by Brother Roger on Easter Day in 1949 is an exception.[9] With lifelong vows, and a Rule, written in the silence of a long retreat in the winter of 1952–53 by Brother Roger, the Taizé Community has

6 Murdoch, Iris, 1958, *The Bell*, London: Chatto and Windus.

7 *Lectio Divina* (Latin for 'Divine Reading') is a traditional Benedictine practice of scriptural reading, meditation and prayer intended to promote communion with God and to increase the knowledge of God's Word. It does not treat Scripture as texts to be studied, but as the Living Word. Traditionally, Lectio Divina has four separate steps: read; meditate; pray; contemplate. First a passage of Scripture is read, then its meaning is reflected upon. This is followed by prayer and contemplation on the Word of God. From https://en.wikipedia.org/wiki/Lectio_Divina (accessed 5 February 2022).

8 Murdoch, Iris, 2004, *The Bell*, reprint, London: Vintage, p. 139.

9 See https://www.taize.fr/en_article6526.html (accessed 5 February 2022).

continued to flourish despite Roger's tragic and violent murder over 15 years ago. Highly significant is the requirement that the brothers make lifelong vows which enable them to offer the stability needed to transcend the founder's influence, as they continue to influence deeply the spirituality of generations of young people.

A Household of Faith: 'a patterne for an adge that needs patternes'

Eliot was mindful of the tradition of Little Gidding, stretching back to the time of Nicholas Ferrar who, in 1625, following his family's financial collapse, established an intentional household of faith at the manor house there. He relocated his mother, sister and brother, and their families, and devised a way of life based on devotion, order and education that lasted a couple of decades, and drew in a 'web of friendships', held together by Ferrar's leadership and counsel. He ruled the household with authority, which included others beyond the immediate family, amounting to 30 or 40 residents; each was required to accept a Rule of life with explicit written promises.[10] Ferrar intended that the community become 'a light on a hill' for society around – 'a patterne for an adge that needs patternes.'[11] With the advice of his close friend George Herbert, he devised a daily round of morning and evening prayer, Sunday worship, and catechizing according to the *Book of Common Prayer*, with additional vigils during the night for those who were happy to volunteer. Ferrar claimed that 'the best minds are like clocks which to goe right need daily winding upp',[12] not only by an ordered prayer life, but also a small school for the local children, paying them a penny for each psalm they could recite. All were occupied with active practical work routines and husbandry; the arts, particularly embroidery, and conversation to go with it, were encouraged; hospitality was offered to all who came; and

10 See Ransome, Joyce, 2011, *The Web of Friendship*, Cambridge: James Clarke and Co., p. 110.

11 Ransome, *Web of Friendship*, p. 176.

12 Ransome, *Web of Friendship*, p. 64.

with Ferrar's medical training, health care and dietary advice or 'temperance', was also on offer to the local community. On the whole, it seems most were happy to accept Ferrar's authority, except, notably, Bathsheba, the wife of his brother John, who pined for London with a vengeance, and his sister Susanna Collet who, with her family, had extended times away.

Mary Ferrar, Ferrar's mother, led the 'Little Academy' which cultivated conversation and promoted the education of the women and girls. The women also made elaborate 'Harmonies' of the books and Gospels of the Bible, integrating the texts into a continuous narrative. Thirteen of these were created, and were sought after, not least by King Charles I, who visited Little Gidding three times. Indeed, he was harboured there, later, as he fled from the battle of Naseby, the 'broken king' of Eliot's poem, who came at night, to find friendship and hospitality in the midst of turmoil. The community lasted beyond Nicholas' death in 1637, led by his siblings until they both died in 1657, surviving the Civil War, the execution of Charles I, and the establishment of the Commonwealth under Cromwell.

The Ferrar household was an experiment that helped generate a particular Anglican spirituality. Ferrar associated closely with George Herbert, sharing a devotional spirit that was expressed in Herbert's *The Country Parson*, and is described thus by Izaac Walton:

> Mr Farrers, and Mr Herberts devout lives, were both so noted, that the general report of their sanctity gave them occasion to renew that slight acquaintance which was begun at their being Contemporaries in Cambridge; and this new holy friendship was long maintain'd without any interview, but only by loving and endearing Letters.[13]

Theirs was the same spirit of *via media*, in a national Church torn between the heavy-handed uniformity imposed by Archbishop Laud and the Puritan swing to individual piety, predestination and protest. Herbert had responsibility for the

13 Walton, Izaak, 1927, *Lives*, edited by Humphrey Milford, Oxford: Oxford University Press, p. 312.

neighbouring parish of Leighton Bromswold, and asked the Ferrars to renovate the church, where two pulpits were installed to emphasize the equality of the Word, prayed and preached. Today, each May, a pilgrimage snakes its way from Leighton Bromswold to Little Gidding, recalling the abiding friendship between Ferrar and Herbert. When Herbert died in 1633, prematurely of tuberculosis, he left his poems to Ferrar, who took responsibility for their publication during the last years of his own life, and so we have Herbert's poems today.

The Little Gidding community attracted adverse attention from the Puritans, who threatened the place, surrounding it with malicious rumours, including an attack entitled *An Arminian Nunnery*.[14] The Bishop of Lincoln, John Williams, warned the Ferrars not to prefix letters with the Jesuit-associated Christogram 'HIS', for fear of stirring further Puritan antipathy. The denigrating gossip was keenly felt, as Mary Ferrar's warning to visitors suggests:

> He who [by reproof of our errors and remonstrance of that which is more perfect] seeks to make us better, is welcome as an angel of God – *and* – He who (by a cheerful participation and approbation of that which is good) confirms us in the same, is welcome as a Christian Friend.
>
> *But*
>
> He who any ways goes about to disturb us in that which is and ought to be among Christians (tho' it be not usual in the world) is a burden while he stays and shall bear his judgment whosoever he be – *and* – He who faults us in absence for that which in presence he makes show to approve of, doth by a double guilt of flattery and slander violate the bands both of friendship and charity.[15]

14 Lenton, Edward, 1987, *An Arminian Nunnery. Or, A Brief Description and Relation of the Late Erected Monastical Place, Called the Arminian Nunnery at Little Gidding in Huntington-shire*, originally published 1641, Little Gidding: Little Gidding Books.

15 See Maycock, A. L., 1938, *Nicholas Ferrar of Little Gidding*, London, SPCK, p. 149.

This 'intentional community', then, was sustained during an age of national turmoil, and its inspiration has continued. Ransome is thus probably right to see Ferrar's founding of the Little Gidding community as an influence on subsequent voluntary associations and societies within the Anglican Church.[16] What was remarkable was Ferrar's self-conscious intentionality in forming his household, with an order and disciplined devotion that he hoped would have a wider impact to ameliorate society around. It has left its legacy in shaping the spirituality of the Church of England in following centuries.[17]

The Twentieth Century at Little Gidding: A 'Spiritual Powerhouse'?

Little Gidding attracted renewed attention in the 1930s. After T. S. Eliot's visit, Alan Maycock, the librarian of Magdalene College, Cambridge, where many of the Ferrar papers are held, wrote a biography of Ferrar, in which he expressed the dream that one day a community would be re-established at Little Gidding to become 'a spiritual powerhouse from which the Church and her children may draw strength.'[18] The Friends of Little Gidding, founded in 1947, continued to build support and interest in the place, and in 1969 the Little Gidding Fellowship was formed to pray for the realization of this dream. Tony and Judith Hodgson bought the freehold of Manor Farm (a nineteenth-century farmhouse built on the site of the original manor house that was destroyed by fire in 1810), with eight acres, along with the old farm buildings. During the next four years a community formed around them, offering hospitality, with work-camps, conferences and retreats. Communal life was based on three principles: a welcome to all who came across the threshold; the development of a way of prayer that was rooted in tradition, but also relevant to the needs of today's world;

16 Ransome, *Web of Friendship*, p. 192.

17 See Ransome, *Web of Friendship*, ch. 7.

18 Maycock, *Nicholas Ferrar*, p. 305

and the need to love and respect all God's gifts in creation.[19] Hodgson writes of the vision and tensions of those four years, and explains with perhaps characteristic self-effacement, that 'both the seventeenth-century and the twentieth-century communities come to an end through human wilfulness',[20] seeming to blame himself, as leader, for a lack of time spent praying.

In 1976 Robert and Sarah Van der Weyer moved to Little Gidding and raised enough money in 1977 for a new Charitable Trust to purchase the farmhouse, its outbuildings and the eight acres of land. Van der Weyer gathered a community around himself, with most living in the houses that were built or converted from the outbuildings. The community took the name of 'The Community of Christ the Sower', and was made up of families and single people of all ages and different denominations. In 1985 the Van der Weyers also bought the old manor house at Leighton Bromswold, and members lived in various houses in the village, with guests in a community house. During the 1980s and 1990s several families made homes in the converted farm buildings, following the guidelines for communal life laid down by Van de Weyer. Members were invited to commit themselves initially for a year. This commitment included an expectation, so far as it was possible, for them to attend daily prayers with the rest of the community, and to share a weekly common meal and a Communion service which was usually on a Saturday night to free people for Sunday worship in parish churches around.

Something of the culture of this community is evident in *The Little Gidding Way: Christian Community for Ordinary People*, published in 1988. Van der Weyer observes that communal living has always been part of the Christian witness, and now:

> although the essence of Christian community never changes, its outward expression is constantly evolving; and today the call to community is being heard more widely than ever before. In the past only a tiny minority of Christians have belonged to communities; today the movement towards com-

19 See Hodgson, Tony, 2010, *Little Gidding Then and Now*, Grove Books: Cambridge.

20 Hodgson, *Little Gidding Then and Now*, p. 6.

> munity seems to be stirring people throughout the Church, and is in all sorts of ways – seen and unseen, large and small – affecting people's way of life and worship.[21]

As Van der Weyer outlined, the communal life of Christ the Sower was not to be governed by a strict rule in the monastic sense, but by four aspects of the vision: covenant, stewardship, ministry and reconciliation, which he elucidates in *The Little Gidding Way*. A companion prayer book, which followed its own cycle of biblical readings, was also produced to support lay people seeking to live alongside, or in association with the community.[22]

The Community of Christ the Sower lasted into the 1990s and came to an end with a lengthy and painful legal case, after which a new Charitable Trust was established that continues today with the sole object of 'the Advancement of Religion particularly by Pilgrimages to the Church at Little Gidding.'[23] The current trustees now manage the properties, and continue the tradition of hospitality at Ferrar House, particularly for pilgrims and retreatants. The Friends of Little Gidding flourish, overseeing an annual pilgrimage in May, the Nicholas Ferrar Day on the first Saturday of December, and the T. S. Eliot Festival (founded in 2006), annually in July. There is no current plan to create any form of community at Little Gidding again.

With its mixture of intention and self-conscious devotion, the Ferrar vision was an experiment in Anglican spirituality, offering something new and different in the seventeenth century which in turn inspired the communities of the 1970s. As forms of 'new monasticism'[24] emerge in today's Church of England,

---

21 Van de Weyer, Robert, 1988, *The Little Gidding Way*, London: Darton, Longman and Todd, pp. 3–4.

22 Van de Weyer, Robert, 1986, *The Little Gidding Prayer Book*, London: SPCK, p. 4.

23 The Little Gidding Trust Ltd, charity number 1105821.

24 As already described and discussed at some length in Chapter 8 of this book, 'new monasticism' is the term used to describe contemporary intentional communities which seek to re-interpret the vision to live communally in today's world. The term was seemingly first used in 1998 by Jonathan R. Wilson in his book *Living Faithfully in a Fragmented World: Lessons for the Church from Macintyre's After Virtue*, Edinburgh, T &T Clark.

what might be learned from Nicholas Ferrar's experiment in communal life, and subsequent attempts to create community at Little Gidding?

Themes of leadership and motivation, or intentionality, come first to mind. Second, what of the significance of place and belonging, and the seemingly nostalgic or utopian impulse that continues to draw people on pilgrimage to places like Little Gidding? Then, what of the ordering of time and activity that shapes communal life? The legacy of Little Gidding, the place and the poem, is worth considering again by those seeking to live intentionally in community today.

Leadership: 'This is the right, good, old way; keep in it'

Ferrar took leadership seriously.[25] He established the pattern of daily prayer, and the routines of daily life, ruling the community with clarity of decision and sound advice and guidance. He was pivotal; the original household existed for 20 years after he died, but cannot really be said to have established itself independently of his will and purpose. 'This is the right, good old way', he said to his brother as he died: 'keep in it'. The two twentieth-century experiments, likewise, revolved around individual leaders, and did not survive beyond their personal influence.

Perhaps the most salient lesson to be learned from the Little Gidding experience is to contrast this style of charismatic, visionary leader with the undertaking of monastic Religious communities ('old' rather than 'new'), where the community carries forward its traditions and elects its leader from among its number. The Rule of St Benedict, ch. 64, says:

25 Ransome's approach differs from other biographies and narratives about the Ferrar household in her reluctance to 'sanctify' Nicholas. In contrast, Alan Maycock is adulatory in his (1938) *Nicholas Ferrar of Little Gidding*, London, SPCK; and much earlier, in the seventeenth century, Bishop Francis Turner, basing his assessment on John Ferrar's retrospective account, was full of praise. Ransome is more inclined to see Ferrar's authoritarian side, which so antagonized his sister-in-law, Bathsheba.

> In choosing an abbot, the guiding principle should always be that the man placed in office be the one selected either by the whole community acting unanimously in the fear of God, or by some part of the community, no matter how small, which possesses sounder judgment. Goodness of life and wisdom in teaching must be the criteria for choosing the one to be made abbot, even if he is the last in community rank. May God forbid that a whole community should conspire to elect a man who goes along with its own evil ways.

This Benedictine tradition of electing a leader works in the ('old') monastic way, where the community pre-exists the leader, who is elected from among the members.[26] The way of life is traditional in the sense that it is passed on through generations of members who concur and accept the rules and practices that have developed over time. By contrast, it is a peculiarly modern phenomenon to form a community around the intention of an individual or small group, and then attempt to sustain that community on a voluntarist basis. The monastic way gives a much greater role to tradition, to that which is handed on as a way of life, instituted and governed. Arguably, this is a more resilient basis for community than that founded by a charismatic leader who relies wholly on the assent and will of the community. When a lay person joins a traditional community as a member of a third order, or as an oblate, they are choosing to participate in this traditional life, deliberately valuing the sense of obedience and regularity that is offered.

The leader of the intentional community, however, without the proper checks and balances to their authority – or to their weakness – can exert a dangerous influence, as Murdoch explored so powerfully in her novel *The Bell*. The novel contrasts both kinds of community: the new and intentional, on the one hand, and the vowed life, on the other – represented by the convent of enclosed nuns, living a short distance away. This vowed community is presented positively – particularly

26 Memorably, in *Of Gods and Men*, the 2010 French drama film about the martyred Cistercian monks of Tibhirine, Algeria, directed by Xavier Beauvois, the monks say to the abbot at one point: 'We did not elect you to make decisions for us.'

by Mother Clare, who dramatically strips herself of her habit to her underwear at one stage, swimming strongly to rescue another character from drowning. For the vowed community is presented as a place where a new postulant or oblate will seek to *test* a Religious vocation, knowing that the tradition of prayer and the way of life they enter is larger than they are; this is a way of life that extends into the past, and through the present into the future. This is a place where time is structured by hours, shaped to form and transform the individual through conformity. In contrast, intentional communities begin and end with the willing individual who joins for any number of reasons, but not usually to lose themselves in a way of life that calls for the risky renunciation of the self into a whole that is greater than the sum of the parts; this is the place where vows made for life truly matter.

There is a key tension here, of course, about *trust*, especially when so many communities, both intentional and monastic, have proved to have untrustworthy cultures, where abuse happens with terrible psychological and physical suffering. It is easy to see why people are reluctant to commit themselves to a way of life which calls for the surrender of personal autonomy. Little Gidding, too, has proved that experiments in intentional communal living are fraught, and they cast long shadows when things go wrong. On the whole, 'old' Religious orders will have struggled with these issues for centuries, and will tend to distrust the charismatic or dominant leadership of one figure alone.

Place: A 'tiny corner of God's earth'

In the poem, T. S. Eliot explored two abiding preoccupations of modernity sparked by his visit to Little Gidding, and the way the place remained in his imagination: these are space and time. If modernity means the dissolving of form, the forgetting of traditions and history, then how is belonging and identity still to happen?

> A people without history
> Is not redeemed from time, for history is a pattern
> Of timeless moments. So, while the light fails
> On a winter's afternoon, in a secluded chapel
> History is now and England.

Andrew Rumsey reminds us of the comment of the French cultural critic Michel Foucault that *time* was modernity's 'great obsession': 'the era when, in myriad ways – steam travel, imperial expansion, a fixation with the myth of progress – the clock conquered the map. Space, perceived as a static commodity, was something to contain and overcome; time, by contrast, was dynamic, the engine of social development and advance'. So Rumsey writes.[27] However, he says, it was space, not time, that emerged as the grand cause of the postmodern worldview. Eliot's quartet, however, ponders both. What can Little Gidding signify about place, if it matters as Rumsey commends? And what of time and history? Is the ordering of time important? Consideration of time and place bring us back to the way in which 'old' monastic orders have understood themselves, and used tradition to form and transform the human person by negotiating the relationship of the individual within the corporate over time and in particular place. The intentional communities at Little Gidding – both of the seventeenth and twentieth centuries – were arguably never going to work on a long-term basis. But because the original Ferrar household happened, Little Gidding now has significance through time as an imagined community with its own religious and cultural traditions. This significance has a positive on-going life, as pilgrims come and go; but not, it seems, as a place of *sustained* potential community. Its significance is thus hard to pinpoint. Paul Handley, who lived there during the time of the Community of Christ the Sower, writes:

> it simply persists – and has endured throughout a history of dull husbandry, religious enthusiasm, wistful tourism, youthful idealism; not a particularly welcoming place, nor a place

27 Rumsey, *The Parish*, p. 70.

> hostile to visitors, but a place that combines indifference with an acceptance of a greater sense of significance and meaning that is largely, perhaps entirely, projected upon it – thanks to Eliot. A peculiar history, its remoteness (a side road off a side road), and its unexpectedness . . . and perhaps this is why it can lay claim to being quintessentially English: all our most significant landscape, locations, views tend to be manufactured at some point and some way. They are places we bring memory to – both our own and the memory of others that we have appropriated.[28]

As Little Gidding has accrued such layers of meaning, it seems to have become somewhere 'sacramental', in a wide and evocative sense.

Rumsey speaks of how such layers develop significance as they grow in the imagination. He reminds his reader of the work of the political scientist Benedict Anderson who wrote: 'All communities are to be distinguished ... by the style in which they are imagined.'[29] Rumsey has the parish under consideration, with its ancient origins and on-going vitality as a place where people belong; but much of what he says can apply to Little Gidding too. He argues that the tradition of a place grows as it is formed by imagination, deepening over time: 'The longer we abide in a place, however, the deeper (and thus more 'traditional') it becomes: growing a texture of meaning and personal association.'[30] As people come, again and again, to Little Gidding, partly they seek to retreat, to escape, which always has the dangers of nostalgia, or utopianism. But alternatively, as Rumsey claims, nostalgia and utopianism can lead to other meanings that transcends human signification, where reality is found in God-made-incarnate in Jesus Christ. He echoes John Inge's *A Christian Theology of Place*[31]: 'For Inge, a Christian understanding of place has a sacramental quality that

28 Personal correspondence.
29 Rumsey, *The Parish*, p. 76.
30 Rumsey, *The Parish*, p. 31.
31 Inge, John, 2016, *A Christian Theology of Place*, London: Routledge.

stems from his doctrinal conviction that, in Jesus Christ, created space-time becomes imbued with the presence of God.'[32]

Little Gidding offers an intense engagement with the traditions of a place which throws into relief our modernist/post-modernist condition where we can be at danger of losing ourselves and our ultimate place – in the world, but also not of the world:

> The idea of an ultimate place introduces hope and perspective into local practice. Consciously or unconsciously, we enact our understanding not only of the places we presently live in but also the places to which we aspire. It is therefore in place that we receive the call beyond our existing situation to possible future locations, meaning that hopeful action in any locale requires a degree of faithfulness to a vision of how our place might one day be: such faith being the motor of all political and moral change in society, utopian or otherwise.[33]

Over the door to the church at Little Gidding are inscribed words from Gen. 28.17: 'This is none other but the house of God and the gate of heaven', which prompted Tony Hodgson to say of Little Gidding that it 'stands for the wideness of God's mercy and the depth of God's love, rooted in a tiny corner of God's earth which is, "England and nowhere"'.[34] If earthly place is perceived sacramentally as the 'gate of heaven', then it is a sacrament of Christ's local presence, according to Rumsey,[35] where the nostalgic finds relevant meaning and the utopian comes to rest in particularity. Here dreams and shadows take on the full force of reality, the weight of glory.

Rumsey is led to conclude that the Anglican covenant with place is instinctive, *given*, and surprisingly hard to articulate, particularly in a world and society that longs for roots while simultaneously denying them.[36] He argues that the Church of England could be bolder in asserting its genius for place, and

32 Rumsey, *The Parish*, p. 11.
33 Rumsey, *The Parish*, p. 32.
34 Quote in Hodgson, *Web of Friendship*, p. 25.
35 Rumsey, *The Parish*, p. 49.
36 Rumsey, *The Parish*, p. 67.

how certain places absorb and embody belief.[37] To do this, one needs to take seriously the narratives of the past, including nostalgic ones:

> The assumed narrative of nostalgia is that its redundancy – and therefore its ripeness for parody and dismissal – arises from the impossibility of return. Because it attempts to recreate a fictional past, nostalgia is commonly portrayed as deliberately ignorant: a denial of history. *And did those feet in ancient time? No, therefore* (the assumption often goes) – *end of story*. I would argue that, especially in its contemporary form, parochial nostalgia – the desire for homeland, or the longing to belong – manifests itself far more dynamically as a highly significant component in place-formation.[38]

Not only does this have consequences for a sense of belonging and identity for those who live in the parish but, Rumsey says, 'such imaginative geographies (past and future-orientated) have successively proved to be engines of resistance to versions of the present "problematic" place'.[39] One of the potential lessons of Little Gidding, then – and of other places of national pilgrimage such as 'old' monastic abbeys and communities – is a reminder of the importance of place to inspire belonging, and so also dreams and hopes for a better world. Many parish groups already visit Little Gidding; what's to stop such groups inviting local neighbours from other faiths to join them on a pilgrimage, better to reflect on their own shared journeys and homes? Reflection on the history and poetry of that place, why it inspires and what the shadows have been, can enable reflection on what 'belonging' means today in any context. Pilgrimage is widely understood across different religions and faith groups, and can offer much to feed the processes of re-imagination in local communities, especially of belonging and identity. Rumsey's words here can apply as well, if not better, to Little Gidding as to the parish; for it is when people are most

37 Rumsey, *The Parish*, p. 68.
38 Rumsey, *The Parish*, p. 169.
39 Rumsey, *The Parish*, p. 169.

prepared to give up their sense of ultimate claim to a place that *new* ways of belonging can emerge:

> The vocation of the Anglican parish is, therefore, to give spatio-temporal expression to the 'new place' in the midst of the old – a task that, crucially, involves the demotion of past and present places from their claim to ultimacy, which is the very root of territorial idolatry.[40]

Rumsey's thoughtful account of the parish is profound. He calls for 'a lively apprehension of the work of the Holy Spirit'[41] to enable place to become sacramental of Christ. He says this happens when those who belong, or who seek to possess the land, are prepared 'relinquish' it, to 'give up one's place' for God and neighbour in order to receive afresh 'in the kingdom':

> This is an eminently hopeful calling, offering both resolution of nostalgia and release from the idolatry of homeland, to which the parochial tradition is chronically prone. While it does not satiate the 'longing for home' – indeed *separation* is the inevitable corollary of our eschatological situation – it does settle and solve this in the conviction that where we belong, finally, is in Christ.[42]

Rumsey thus captures themes of remembering and forgetting, and commends '*anamnesia* – the kind of hopeful remembrance at the core of the Christian gospel.'[43] I don't think this is so far from what Eliot sought in his fourth quartet: a meaningful remembering that consciously inhabits a particular place to enable belonging and identity. Little Gidding is a place that belongs to no one, as such: yet it is a place people feel they belong, as they come again and again, much as pilgrims return to places of pilgrimage over and over, seeking a belonging that offers 'Easter in ordinary', a reminder of the gate of heaven.

40 Rumsey, *The Parish*, p. 171.
41 Rumsey, *The Parish*, p. 172.
42 Rumsey, *The Parish*, p. 173.
43 Rumsey, *The Parish*, p. 182.

As we have seen, imagined communities also have shadows; and if T. S. Eliot identified Little Gidding with England, perhaps there are also lessons here about living with the past, within communities and as a nation. Rumsey suggests that the highly contested discourse of England and Englishness, which is so easily claimed by those who intend a resurgent nationalism across the British Isles, should not be conceded to such people:

> Whenever received wisdom insists ... that social conservatism and attachment to territory are necessarily a symptom of something sinister – then extremism and insularity become self-fulfilling prophecies, being the only lens people are offered to view these allegiances through. England, owing to its imperious role in the formation and governance of the United Kingdom, is chronically prone to this condition – unlike the Scots, for example, whose commitment both to 'Little Scotland' and radical social cohesion is something the English can only watch with envy and a heavy measure of despair.[44]

Some, then, will say that Eliot's exploration of 'Englishness', as he reflected upon it at Little Gidding, is too tainted today. On the other hand, it might be that we are taken, at Little Gidding, right to the heart of a particular 'Englishness' that remembers another age when Nicholas Ferrar and George Herbert made meaning in the midst of religious conflict and turmoil. To remember their time can provide insight to what it means to imagine community – whether it be a nation, a parish, a neighbourhood or a street – into existence, and then live with the conflicts and shadows, allowing the place also to redeem.

T. S. Eliot echoes Julian of Norwich as he concludes that 'all shall be well and all manner of thing shall be well'. The novelist and spiritual director, Charles Williams, writing in 1942 of the forgiveness of sins and whether it is possible for one nation to forgive another nation, says of Julian that 'few, if any, of the English have written so greatly of pardon as she', of the glory of the Atonement, which makes possible the forgiveness of sins. 'It enabled sin to be fully sin, and it fully counteracted

44 Rumsey, *The Parish*, p. 110.

sin.'[45] There is much to be forgiven as the past is recalled in England, given its colonial crimes, begun at the time of Ferrar and Herbert. That past cannot be forgotten, or else it remains unforgiven, unredeemed.

Time, too, is an arena of redemption.

Time: 'the best minds are like clocks which to goe right need daily winding upp'

> History may be servitude,
> History may be freedom. See, now they vanish,
> The faces and places, with the self which, as it could, loved them,
> To become renewed, transfigured, in another pattern.

Malcolm Guite takes these words of Eliot in 'Little Gidding', showing how remembering, 'an art of memory', becomes an 'art of salvation', as Eliot seeks to 'redeem the time', not by escaping it but by transforming it.[46] The transformation is achieved through 'pattern'. The Ferrar household, with its regular pattern of prayer, of reciting the psalms, surely tried to re-establish the patterns of life that had been lost at the dissolution of the monasteries. In so far as any Religious order regulates its life with communal patterns of prayer and activity, then it both creates and joins with patterns of prayer and worship that shape the individual into something bigger and ultimately redemptive. Time, when patterned with calendar and routine, becomes meaningful, as movement becomes meaningful as dance:

> From wrong to wrong the exasperated spirit
> Proceeds, unless restored by that refining fire
> Where you must move in measure, like a dancer.

45 Williams, Charles, 1984, *The Forgiveness of Sins*, originally published 1942, Grand Rapids, Eerdmans, pp. 99–100.

46 In *The Journal of the T. S. Eliot Society (UK)*, (2013), pp. 1–14.

The disciplines of ordered prayer, such that the individual can do no other than be conformed to that practice, is the beginning of the redemption of time. When one agrees, voluntarily, to submit to the disciplines of the daily office, or to join a third order, for example, there freedom is found. St Augustine knew this: perfect freedom is found in service; and what is more real than the service of God in prayer? In so far as Ferrar perceived this, his intentional community found 'the right, good, old way'. Here, the individual both loses self and finds self, as he or she agrees to submit to the givenness of a day ordered by prayer, in a communal life that is physically present, or understood as the communion of saints – the company of voices that transcend time and space. To vow oneself to this life is to find a life that is stronger than death. In so far as traditional Religious communities seek to sustain the disciplines and rhythms of prayer and communal life, shaping themselves to a different construction of time, so they witness to an enduring way of life that finds a freedom in regularity, a freedom which is also a freedom from aberrant choice and license. To live in time in such a way can be to see it as sacramental.

Conclusion

In conclusion, this chapter has wondered at the abiding appeal of Little Gidding. Why has it continued as a pilgrimage destination, that attracts people back again and again? The story of Nicholas Ferrar and his experiment in community, with his deep Anglican devotion and structured life, leaves the pilgrim today once more imagining the seventeenth century, with all its turbulence and turmoil. Ferrar's intentional community, as a longed-for oasis of calm and regularity, yet with its internal tensions caused in no small part by his authoritarian leadership, leaves one with a rich insight into the early days of Anglican devotional spirituality and religious practice. These complex layers were made explicit as T. S. Eliot offered poetic reflection on the nature of the human need for roots in place, particularly in his own 1940s world of death, transience and ruptured existence. His extended meditation on the relation of time and place continues to bear meaning for those who visit Little Gidding today, such that they often say that they return to their homes with an enriched understanding of their place in the world. Little Gidding engages the imagination, and tells its story, making time and space meaningful, reminding the pilgrim of the importance of belonging, of roots to identity. I have suggested that both time and place become sacramental, and redemptive, when each is taken and given a sense of living tradition with power to shape the individual into belonging in a way more abiding and enduring than the 'world' can give us. Places with history, or with regulated time, offer the experience of pilgrimage, the promise of Religious community, and they show us once more the vowed life as 'Easter in ordinary': a moment when religious practice is a serious participation in the grace of God.

Alex Evans writes that we need myths and stories more than ever today to 'enable' the imagined communities to which we belong.[47] This is particularly true in these straitened times, as it proves difficult to imagine what it might be like to belong to a global community, given the strength of tribal belonging and the questioning, even fragmentation, of national identities, not least, here in the UK. As the world faces real challenges and requires strong myths to draw together disparate and often conflicted groups and communities, part of that process could include the story of Little Gidding with its lessons of the dangers of charismatic leadership, and more positively, the importance of remembering and gathering, of place and time, to draw us to the redemption that liberates us from meaninglessness, and from the guilt-ridden hold of history:

> A people without history
> Is not redeemed from time, for history is a pattern
> Of timeless moments. So, while the light fails
> On a winter's afternoon, in a secluded chapel
> History is now and England.

47 Evans, Alex, 2017, *The Myth Gap: What Happens when Evidence and Arguments aren't Enough?*, London: Eden Project Books.

10

Evangelical Monasticism: A Not-So-Strange Sympathy

RICHARD SUDWORTH

In this chapter Richard Sudworth reflects on the apparently odd sympathy between evangelicalism and monastic tradition, one founded in attention to the proper place of prayer, discipline and silence in any authentic approach to mission and witness in the parish context. Writing from inner-city Birmingham and from deep engagement with contemporary British Islam there, Sudworth underscores the spiritual importance of Christian 'monastic' endeavours, both old and new, and their continuing significance for the regeneration of parish life, even when – especially when – such institutions seem to be crumbling.

> Nothing from old times will meet our exigencies. We want a rule which shall answer to the complexity of our own age. We want a discipline which shall combine the sovereignty of soul of Antony, the social devotion of Benedict, the humble love of Francis, the matchless energy of the Jesuits, with faith that fears no trial, with hopes that fears no darkness, with truth that fears no light. (B. F. Westcott)[1]

In this chapter I intend to share some personal reflections on the curious and often ambivalent relationship between evangelicalism and Religious orders. I want to suggest a brief 'thinking aloud' about the Religious life's persistent appeal to evangel-

1 Westcott, Brooke Foss, 1902, *Words of Faith and Hope*, New York: Macmillan and Company, p. 14.

ical clergy and what it might tell us in turn about the nature of the Anglican priesthood and mission today. This volume points to some of the exciting new monastic ventures that have been birthed from evangelical traditions, not least our own Archbishop Justin Welby's pioneering of the Community of St Anselm at Lambeth Palace. What then is it about Religious orders, the vowed life, that is so compelling to evangelicals?

This is a question I ask of myself, acknowledging an evangelical-charismatic spirituality that has, in recent years, been further shaped by the Jesuits in my research pursuits at Heythrop College and by the wisdom of the Religious in retreats. I look back at my younger self and can only smile at the caricature I used to have, that is not uncommon among evangelicals: of Religious orders being somehow full of irrelevant escapists, living out a life away from the 'real world' and subject to the oppressive legalism of a vowed life. I will come back to this misnomer of the 'real world', but suffice it to say that the context of parish life, its ebbs and flows and the particularities of mission and ministry in inner-city Birmingham, have undermined this crude binary of 'real' and 'unreal'.

While Anglican identity may seem to be creaking and splintering in so many ways, in the resourcing for prayer and contemplation there are telling convergences and complementarities. Evangelical clergy like myself will readily take retreats in monastic institutions and practise silence, while still being fuelled by guitar-led Sunday worship. Let us not forget, too, that the daily office to which a priest commits is itself a carry-over of the monastic patterns of the divine office, or as the Benedictine traditions terms it, the 'Work of God'. The vowed life of priesthood already promises me to a pattern of worship and prayer – a trajectory that cannot but nudge me towards a community and a tradition beyond myself. My natural instincts as an evangelical towards activism and proclamation, towards the joys of conversion and discipleship, do not diminish as I witness as a parish priest! However, coming from a context where over 80% of my parishioners are Muslim, and churches within inner-city Birmingham face very real threats to the sustainability of their future presence, those instincts in me need to be undergirded by a spirituality that can encompass God's hiddenness. When presiding at a Eucharist for just twenty or so communicants, conscious of the bills that need to be paid and the diocesan share that *cannot* be paid, the gift that is the liturgy becomes the place where the priest becomes dependent upon the prior work of God and is not subject to the tyranny of success. To put it more crudely, I have been thrown back on the patterns of worship that exhibit and resonate with a contemplative temper in order to maintain a presence that can be mission-minded. In a context of ecclesial fragility I see in myself very evident temptations to 'make something happen'; I feel the pressure to somehow manufacture the experience of encounter with God from amidst the surrounding vista of apparent decline. The 'good' evangelical sensibilities of vibrant teaching and contextualized worship can become too easily freighted by my own messianic delusions.

Instead, to enter a space that is already given by God, and speaks from beyond the visible signs of this particular institution or parish church, frames and nourishes the priestly vocation. So, the practice of silence fostered within the vowed life of the Religious speaks eloquently into the silence of our half-empty, cavernous churches. That there exist communities of men and women committed for life to continuous prayer sets a palpable context from which to minister as a parish priest. The 'strangeness' of Religious communities asserts defiantly that the Christian life is characterized by an essential 'homelessness in the world'.[2] This strangeness has its pale echo in patient, priestly ministry among congregations where unemployment and mental illness are commonplace. It is the strangeness of human flourishing from within the gift of God that is aslant to a society in hock to power, success and wealth. I believe this is one of the reasons for the persistent appeal of the Religious to the evangelical tradition: it speaks prophetically of the penultimate nature of the Church. Ever conscious of the potentially deadening impact of organized religion on spiritual life, the vowed life acts as a counterpoint to our self-pretensions as

2 Williams, Rowan, 2011, 'The Only Real City: Monasticism and the Social Vision', in *A Silent Action: Engagements with Thomas Merton*, Louisville, KY: Fons Vitae, pp. 55–68, at p. 64.

priests. We will never pray enough, evangelize enough, be holy enough; only God is 'enough'.

The paradox is, as evangelicals embracing the prophetic gift of the Religious in spiritual direction and in contemplative practices, we find ourselves face to face with our catholic brothers and sisters, and indeed to the undivided Church of the East and West. I wonder that the loosening of ministerial anxiety that comes from an encounter with the contemplative life of the Religious actually loosens our ecclesial anxiety. I am reminded of the late Seamus Heaney who wrote of the palpable pull of the mystery of the Eucharist as 'an undying/tremor and draw, like well water far down'.[3] We literally cannot help ourselves; there is well water, far down, within the inheritance of the Religious that goes beyond the ecclesial fads and fashions that we can all be a slave to.

Another significant dimension for my own appreciation of the Religious has been the encounter with Islam. Famously, Islam struggles with the idea of the Religious, often adducing the dictum attributed to Muhammad that 'there is no monasticism in Islam'. For early Muslim mystics who were sensitive to this potential critique they cited the Christian habit of creating human institutions to govern what could only be a matter of divine human providence.[4] What is not in doubt is the Islamic commitment to a discipline of prayer and the public importance of those who give especial attention to the spiritual life. In small matters of wearing clergy attire in the parish and making more obvious the patterns of prayer that we seek to foster in the Church, our Islamic context recognizes the vowed life of Christians as consonant with a fundamental orientation to God.

I recall a visit to a Birmingham parish church by the then bishop John Sentamu. On entering the neighbouring mosque, he dramatically and without prompting or preamble prostrated himself on the floor and stayed in prayer for several minutes

3 Heaney, Seamus, 2006, 'Out of this World' in *District and Circle*, London: Faber & Faber, p. 47.

4 See Griffith, Sidney H., 2005, 'Merton, Massignon, and the Challenge of Islam', in Baker, Rob and Henry, Gray (eds), *Merton & Sufism: The Untold Story, A Complete Compendium*, Louisville, KY: Fons Vitae, pp. 51–78, at p. 51.

before engaging in dialogue with the mosque leaders. The visit still has an imaginative hold on the mosque community and is recounted with awe to this day. They were impacted by the seriousness with which Archbishop Sentamu held prayer: it had a prior claim to dialogue, mission and the civic politics of an interfaith visit. It is this *seriousness* that the Religious life signals especially for evangelicals, and evangelicals that have at times felt the shop-worn nature of easy grace: of discipleship that too readily dispenses with discipline and rigour.

Despite the rhetoric of Islamic tradition about the folly of the Religious, there are parallel stories in the tradition of Muslim encounters with Christian monks as fellow people of prayer, as well as Muslims devoted to lives of contemplation. In my own parish, we have become ever more mindful of the place that prayer must take as a continuous, public activity: prayer as a vowed life for the community. This admission may seem to be a restatement of what should be axiomatic to a church. The reality is, though, that the church's opening to the community in mission carries it with it a re-energizing of our own life in prayer.

I'm fond of commending areas like Sparkbrook to my friends in the suburbs or in rural parishes: 'People *do God* here.' We don't have to lever in a 'God-for-the-gaps' in our conversations with neighbours; our Muslim, Sikh and Hindu parishioners get that prayer underpins a life lived well. The irony is that in our churches we have too often side-lined the contemplative life, half-embarrassed at this vestige of eccentricity. The utter absurdity and eccentricity of Religious communities calls us back to that undergirding in prayer. I have to admit that this has been something of my own lesson in what is best described as a post-secular, religious inner-city parish. Attending community regeneration meetings with various civic stakeholders, it has been the mosque hosts who have decided to begin the meeting in prayer. Invited to the commemoration of Muhammad's birthday, I have been asked to share some words along with a dozen other community representatives and told to 'pray for us, bless us'. I was breaking fast with friends at a Shia mosque during Ramadan earlier in the year and approached by a Muslim woman who had questions about fasting in Christianity: 'You are a priest; you must know about prayer!' At that moment, deep down, I did not feel I knew *anything* about prayer and was humbled by her own passion and devotion for God.

In reflecting on the stimulus to serious spirituality provided by my multi-faith context I am not somehow eliding the sharp differences between faiths; the missionary opening out to the community need not lose any of its vigour. Neither am I suggesting that I can assess what is going on within the religious traditions that I encounter. All that I can attest to is the humble recognition of an openness to God. In Max Warren's celebrated introduction to the Christian Presence series of missionary texts, he suggests that when we encounter another culture, another religion, we 'take off our shoes, for the place we are approaching is holy'. He warns that we may tread on people's dreams and, 'more seriously still, we may forget that God was here before our arrival'.[5] The life of prayer that is modelled by the Religious is not about conjuring up God, indeed may be deliberately 'making nothing happen'.[6] The cessation of activity, the stillness and the silence, become opportunities to rediscover our dependence, our beloved-ness in God's sight. We join with the vowed Religious in those moments to recognize the ultimate orientation of our lives and the source of any goodness and grace that may exist in our busyness and strivings. What should not surprise us is that God is already at work, already loving, and that people of other faiths and none are resonating with the seriousness of prayer.

I think that it is telling that Warren uses sacramental language to describe this interreligious encounter, evocative of Moses and the burning bush – of a place set apart for encounter with God. My own low-church sensibilities baulk at the idea of 'sacred space' but there *is* something about reserving place for

5 Warren, Max, 1959, 'General Introduction' in Cragg, Kenneth, *Sandals at the Mosque: Christian Presence Amid Islam*, London: SCM, pp. 9–10.

6 A phrase borrowed from W. H. Auden's *In Memory of W. B. Yeats*: 'For poetry makes nothing happen' (Auden, W. H., 1976, *Collected Poems*, edited by Edward Mendelson, London: Faber & Faber, p. 248.). See D'Costa, Gavin, Nesbitt, Eleanor, Pryce, Mark, Shelton, Ruth and Slee, Nicola, 2014, *Making Nothing Happen: Five Poets Explore Faith and Spirituality*, London: Routledge; and also the poetry addendum to this volume, below.

prayer. My own Muslim neighbours, strictly speaking, have no theology of sacred space yet instinctively guard physical space for prayer and recognize and respect those spaces in churches. One of the great joys in visiting convents and monasteries on retreat is the almost tangible sense that prayer has been concentrated and held in those places often for hundreds of years. Our parish church is a modern community building with glass walls and a downstairs café area; its functionalism is a far cry from the history and beauty of Little Gidding! But I have lost count of the numbers of Muslims, Sikhs and Hindus coming through our doors who will tell me how peaceful and prayerful the church seems. Rhythms of prayer *in this place* are what animate our encounter with the community, as they do in Little Gidding and countless other churches with or without their transcendent beauty.

Here in Birmingham there has been a constant witness of the Christian vowed life in the community of St John the Divine in nearby Alum Rock. Made famous by the *Call the Midwife* television series, this is an order that has committed to working alongside women in areas of urban deprivation, first in the East End but latterly in inner-city Birmingham. Alum Rock, like Sparkbrook, is now a Muslim-majority parish that testifies to the loving and prayerful service of this Religious order. A dwindling and ageing Religious community has meant that the doors of St John the Divine have had to close. Many clergy and lay Christians have found support and direction from the nuns over the years. However, it is plain to see the paradox that at a time of resurgent interest in the Religious life, many orders are struggling to recruit and facing challenges of financial sustainability. There is a particular charism in the vowed life of Religious orders that is evidently at risk even as we welcome creative re-imaginings of prayerful communities. The good news for Alum Rock is that the site has been bought by a missionary organization that intends to continue the legacy of public service, prayer and hospitality.

The likely contribution of this new witness to prayer in Birmingham is unclear. In many ways, the Alum Rock story encapsulates both the energy and uncertainty of our current situation. The future of many Religious orders remains fragile while creative and innovative ventures that are reinvigorating committed, communal prayer are springing up. From evangelical-charismatic dispersed communities like the St Thomas Sheffield network, to the continuing experiment of the Moot community in the city of London, there are no 'usual suspects' in the renewal of the Religious life. It is worth recalling Westcott's words about the 'complexity of our own age' and wonder at the even greater complexity now. It is not entirely clear how sustainable many of these new communities will be, even how 'vowed', in the totality of calling in comparison to traditional Religious. What they do reveal, though, is a deep yearning for intentional prayer in community and contemplation that also speaks beyond the boundaries of the Church.

One of the great mysteries for Muslims when they look at the Christian life is the question of what we *do* as Christians. It may seem an odd question but when put against the Muslim practice of prayer five times a day and the formalities of Ramadan and pilgrimage, it makes much more sense. The stock Christian response is something like: 'Well we don't *have* to do anything; it's all about freedom, but of course we want to go to church, and pray, and read the Bible etc etc.' Understandably, many Muslims think that Christians don't pray or are at least very lax about spiritual disciplines. We spend so much of our time in churches effectively dumbing down our witness, making things easy, lowering the threshold so that – as we think – the simple call of Christ can be heard. Much of that is good and understandable. However, the life of the Religious reminds us of the all-consuming vows of baptism on each of us. There are people who want to see that a faith decision is a serious one – that it matters. Whether it is the Muslim who begins to see something more in Jesus and is already committed to a discipline of prayer, or the 'spiritual searcher' drawn into an Ignatian meditation class run by a new monastic community, the Church's proclamation perhaps needs to have the courage to be, in some ways, more *difficult*.

Returning to that odd bifurcation of the supposedly real and unreal worlds that I began with: the truth is that the place of grace in silent prayer, held by God, is the real place of all our longings. That a plethora of new monastic movements should be emerging with messy borrowings across spiritual traditions, evidencing also blurred lines across evangelical and catholic borders, should not be a surprise. Westcott's permission to new forms of Religious life in the Victorian era seems rather prescient to the complexities of our own age.

11

Choosing to be Beholden

VICTORIA JOHNSON

In this final chapter of the book Victoria Johnson probes behind the issue of formal Religious 'vows' to ask about the deeper cultural resistance there may be to being 'beholden' to anything or anyone at all. What does this resistance reveal, and could there be something in it, nonetheless, that still echoes the longing for a final 'stability' in God? Taking some telling examples from both parish and cathedral life, Johnson explores the phenomenon of coming to feel 'beholden' to God in the first place, and thus opened up anew to the seriousness of a public 'vow' that is truly life-changing. The issue of 'vows' thus comes full circle in this chapter, as the seemingly scary demands and disciplines of vows are revealed as rooted in God's prior call and the life-long love affair that this bespeaks.

> He, therefore, is the devout man, who lives no longer to his own will, or the way and spirit of the world, but to the sole will of God, who considers God in everything, who serves God in everything, who makes all the parts of his common life parts of piety, by doing everything in the Name of God, and under such rules as are conformable to His glory.[1]

Even today, one occasionally hears the phrase 'I don't want to be *beholden* to anyone.' Being beholden to someone or something is usually seen as an enslaving, indeed a diminishing

1 Law, William, *A Serious Call to a devout and Holy Life, adapted to the State and Condition of all orders of Christians, by William Law, M.A.*, originally published 1729, London: Griffith Farran Browne, Chapter 1. See https://ccel.org/ccel/law/serious_call/serious_call.ii.html (accessed 5 February 2022).

experience. The word 'beholden', as we have it, is derived from the middle English 'behealden', which means to be under obligation or duty for a favour or gift, and can therefore also be a means of expressing thanksgiving or gratitude.

So we have here an archaic, almost extinct and deeply unfashionable word, which speaks of an archaic and deeply unfashionable idea: that of *being beholden* both in terms of duty and service, and in terms of prior gift, thankfulness and adoration. To be voluntarily under the yoke of anything or anyone in contemporary culture is seemingly an anathema, and thus the word *beholden* is usually to be found within the realm of other equally unattractive words such as discipline, virtue and obedience.

But ever counter to any culture in which they sit, Christian citizens *choose* to live under the divine authority of God, with a sense of obedience and obligation, to be sure, and yet also with a sense of joyfulness, gratitude and love; for they are fashioning their own life-in-the-Spirit, and the life of the world around them, in accordance with – and in response to – the life-changing gift that they have received. There is a desire here to *belong* in a fundamental sense. It is through this service and obedience that perfect freedom is actually found – or so any Christian formed in the traditions of Paul and Augustine would argue.

In this tradition too, *A Serious Call to a Devout and Holy Life*, published by William Law in 1729, is a challenging text which explicates Christian piety and commitment in an extraordinary way. This work influenced the Wesleys, and unashamedly sets out in detail the kind of commitments in terms of piety and practice that are to be expected of those who call themselves Christian. Law was possibly one of those infuriating people who 'talked the talk and walked the walk', or practised what he preached: he was part of the Holy Club in every sense. He was serious about his commitment to faith in a way which might begin to make sense of the notion of a solemn vow. Wherever and however his Christian journey began, it came to fruition and was made manifest in what he said, in what he did, in what he wrote, and in how he lived out every single day. It was an utterly all-consuming vision.

Law understood the demands that a living faith makes on a person's *whole* life, and put forward the idea that we express our faith under such 'rules' as are conformable to the glory of God. This suggests that an active faith requires, or even demands a level of discipline, a level of obedience, and a deep level of 'being beholden' to the will of God – or to paraphrase the words of a nineteenth-century hymn, of being caught up in a love which will not let you go.[2] Once caught up in that kind of love, and once beholden to it, there is certainly no going back; and for some the journey is then marked by entering into a vowed life. At that moment the inner beholden-ness to God is transformed and ratified by a public act of commitment.

But let us now reflect upon a seemingly paradoxical counter-instance of this principle and logic, coming from the parish.

One of my former parishioners had the most incredible and dedicated faith, but one which was also beautifully unaffected. It was a little like what I imagine the relationship between Moses and God to have been like; kindled by fire, Moses was a friend of God.[3] If the Church had to get in the way of that, then so be it. This parishioner wanted to step forward as a churchwarden. It was a gift any vicar would have rejoiced in, because they were incredibly practical and eminently sensible and totally committed too: just what you want in a churchwarden. This parishioner spent hours tending the churchyard, cleaning, painting, fixing, encouraging, supporting and was already as committed a Christian as anyone could be. For instance, it occasionally became clear in the course of conversation that at the beginning of every day, morning prayer was said at home: it was just the way that faith was lived out seriously and devotedly and with discipline.

However, my parishioner hadn't ever been confirmed. You see, here was a person who was already *beholden* to God through their baptism. They had already turned aside and in a sense already fallen in love with God. But for canonical and legal reasons anyone wishing to take on the role of churchwarden had to be confirmed, just as anyone wishing to be

2 'O Love, that wilt not let me go', George Matheson (1842–1906).

3 See Ex 3.1–17 and 33.11.

licensed or ordained would have to be. So, I had to go through (what seemed at the time) the faintly ridiculous process of preparing someone for confirmation, (someone who was so obviously already fully committed to the Christian way of life), simply in order to tick a box. 'What *difference* does this make?' This was the question we had to grapple with together. It was hard to know how to answer it at first, since the whole process felt almost transactional and slightly disturbed me. It felt as if I was meddling with the fire of someone's faith, I was worried I would break it, or the Church would break it; and so I was careful to tread gently, as I didn't want to ruin this precious commitment in any way. Indeed, when I think of many others across the Church of England, and the hours and hours they commit to keeping it going through loving service and practical offerings of time, or talents or money, I realize that in many ways this is how a vow becomes a way of life, or where the way of life has already, implicitly, become a vow. Everything was mingled up together; it was hard to untangle where a vow began, and how being beholden to God was to be transformed into a public promise while also fusing into a legal form of Christian service.

After some serious chats in the vicarage, the confirmation happened and it really was a very moving and significant service for all of us. For it brought this beautiful faith out into the light in a new and significant way. In the years since, the 'vow' of confirmation has not been regretted, it has provided everything that it promised, an adult commitment to faith and a renewal of that baptismal vow where it all began, nor have I ever regretted encouraging anyone into making this commitment. There is no doubt that the public affirmation of baptismal vows somehow caused a faith to blossom even more, and this mystery of the special fruit of confirmation was made manifest for all to see.[4]

Similarly, in the marriage service of the Church of England, as part of the blessing of the marriage, there is a lovely line in one of the prayers which likewise sums up the place of a vow as the *mark* or *seal* of being caught up in a love which will not

4 Alex Hughes reflects in more depth on the importance of this transition in Chapter 3, above.

let you go. The priest addresses God and prays over the couple: 'Let their love for each other be a seal upon their hearts and a crown upon their heads.'[5]

In a broader context, is it possible to think of all vows in this way – as a seal upon the heart and as a crown on the head of a pre-existing relationship with God? This was certainly the case for my parishioner and their journey towards confirmation. When the baptismal vows were reaffirmed at confirmation, there was somehow a unifying of all that had gone before and all that would yet be. It seemed to be both a culmination and a new beginning.

A vow rarely springs up from nowhere. A marriage vow is usually preceded by a long engagement and perhaps an even longer relationship, but it then sets a couple on a whole new adventure together: it confirms and ratifies what has been growing already. An ordination vow, likewise, is the culmination of a discernment process of many years; when you go to the ordination of a friend or family member you are reminded of all that has brought them to this auspicious day, but you also understand that the moment of ordination marks the beginning of a whole new way of being, a whole new way of life, while also gathering together all that has gone before.

So too, a baptism or confirmation comes at the end of a period of catechesis for all those involved, and even if it is an uncomprehending baby who is brought to baptism, the sacrament still marks a thanksgiving for all that has gone before while setting out the hope of what is yet to come.

If it is possible to think of a vow in this way – as a 'seal' and as a 'crown' – can we track back still further to the moment, or moments, where 'beholden-ness' begins, at the very conception of a vow? I have often asked wedding couples and ordination candidates: 'Where did this all begin?' When did they first 'behold' one another, when were they first 'beholden' to God? It is rather like the parable of the seed being scattered on the ground: the farmer sleeps night and day, and the seed sprouts and grows but he does not know how, yet it eventually yields

5 2005, *Common Worship: Pastoral Services*, second edition, London: Church House Publishing, p. 111.

a harvest.[6] If the harvest is the vow, when, where and how is the seed planted?

Behold!

To 'behold', the root from which the word 'beholden' takes shoot, connects us to the idea that when someone looks into the face of God, or hears the sound of God, they are transformed and quickened to live out their lives beyond purely themselves. How many times are we commanded by God and his angels to 'behold!'? It is a word by which we begin to see the world differently. And so it is perhaps in that moment of transfixion, where vision is lifted and insight is gifted, that something new takes root. We enter into a space of *connection*, akin to the moment when God breathed life into Adam, as pictured by Michelangelo in his *Creazione di Adamo*, where the act of creation seems to be prefigured by an intense adoring gaze between creator and created. They 'behold' one another. They are caught up in one another in love, they have a desire for their other. It is within that gaze that the promise is made, the vow is already taken, at least incipiently – eye to eye, heart to heart. It is here that it all begins. Sometimes without words, the seed is sown.

We already catch a forward glimpse of the beatific vision here, and like Dante in his *Divine Comedy*, continue as someone indelibly changed towards a final transfiguration. Dante beheld the light and beauty of God at the end of his journey, but perhaps for some, this is where it all begins? Even though the Christian journey usually begins outwardly with baptism, I want to suggest that actually the wheels are set in motion some time before, with a sense of being 'beholden' to God.

As Christians, we *choose* to live a vowed life, a disciplined life, that is beholden to God, and therefore also beholden to one another in community. And so the concept of beholden-ness as a way *into* a vow, and also as an ongoing confirmation *of* a vow, may be one which has something to say to the Christian

6 See Mark 4.26–29.

community and the living-out of a distinctively Christian vocation in a secular culture or a post-modern condition.

Another way of approaching our question is to ask: how do people fall in love with God? Where does it all begin? How is it kindled? Even a slow-burning, every-day, kind of faith has to begin somewhere with a niggle, or a nudge, or indeed a subtle change of vision; but how is that fragile beginning nurtured and then transformed into a formal vow? Not everyone has a road to Damascus moment with flashing lights and voices and an immediate and life-defining change of heart, although the heart is indeed usually where it begins and ends for all of us. In his *Summa Theologiae*, writing in relation to entry into the Christian life, Thomas Aquinas describes it so: 'a person's heart is moved by the Holy Spirit to believe in and love God, and to repent of his sins' (*Summa Theologiae*, III, q. 66, art. 11, co.). It seems that love, occasioned by the Spirit, is where a vow begins. Love is where we first 'behold', and so become 'beholden'.

However, whenever faith begins and then blossoms, the *out-working* of that faith is the critical question for the Church of today. What does it mean to be a devoted Christian person? What does it mean to be a practising and visible Christian? When someone self-defines or self-nominates as 'a Christian', what does that actually mean? Does it just mean – as is often presumed – that we are 'nice people', or we live an ostensibly 'good' life, or we like Royal Weddings? What are the 'outward and visible signs' of being a practising Christian today in terms of service, worship, prayer and study, and what are the inward and invisible commitments that someone might make to follow this way of life? How is faith to be expressed and lived out in a largely secular society? How, in other words, do we live out a 'vowed life'? How do we, as individuals and as the corporate body of the Church, keep the faith and help others seek it out?

To try and answer these questions I turn now to the most recent context of my ministry – cathedrals.

A Place to Behold, Built on a Vow

Cathedrals always seem as if they have been around forever. They stand firm and resolute in our cities, often making concrete the sign of the cross on the landscape and pointing towards heaven with their steeples and towers. Despite their grandeur, they usually start small, and many, as it turns out, are built upon a vow. York Minster is the most glorious gothic marvel carved from buttery stone. It shimmers in the early evening sunshine and inside it is all alight with an expansive collection of stained glass. It is the largest gothic cathedral in Northern Europe and usually attracts 750,000 visitors each year. It was founded on the site where Paulinus, the Gregorian missionary priest, baptized King Edwin of Deira, the husband of Princess Ethelberga of Kent, in 627. She was a Christian woman and specified that baptism had to be part of the marriage deal, a vow for a vow. To mark the occasion, a small wooden church was built to house the regal baptism of King Edwin, and that small wooden church is known as the 'first' Minster, physically lost to history but the place where it all began. Paulinus baptized many others, among them Hilda of Whitby. The small wooden church was made more permanent with stone and has been further adorned and extended year upon year, to reflect the beauty of holiness and to become a testament to the power of the vow.

Ely Cathedral is a similarly impressive East Anglian edifice: the 'Ship of the Fens'. It is a building of monumental proportions, and it is arguably most beautiful at seven thirty in the morning when you tip-toe in for morning prayer. It too was built on a vow: the vow of St Etheldreda, a seventh-century Saxon princess who decided this would be the place where she would live out her own Christian promises. She had already navigated two (arranged but unconsummated) marriages; but in those days, marriage was less about love (or even avowedness) and more about business. Her third vow and first love was always to God alone, and in the Fens she built her holy house where women and men were drawn to offer their lives completely to Christ in community. She was beholden to God from the beginning and she remained beholden to God to the end.

Much later, and after the ravages of the Vikings, the monastic life was rejuvenated once more under Ethelwold and Dunstan, and using Benedict's Rule, the Cathedral became, once again, a place where vows were lived out day by day. This history echoes around the building in corners, in shadows and in song. Every day a small portion of Benedict's Rule is read at the end of morning prayer, recollecting the little practices of faith born of community which involve attention to the smallest and seemingly most insignificant events of daily living: how much to eat and drink, how to read the psalms, how the kitchen is run, how to tend for the sick and children.

The Rule of St Benedict reminds us all, lest we should feel too aggrandized by the majesty of a building, that living out the Christian life and indeed living out a vow, involves a certain kind of practical domesticity: it affects everything we do, everything we say, everything we think, from dawn until dusk. Just as William Law set out his expectations in *A Serious Call to a Devout and Holy Life* in the eighteenth century, the much older Rule of St Benedict offers a similar vision of Christian community which is all-embracing, and is still an attractive concept to people searching for authenticity and community. Through faith we become beholden not only to God, but to one another.[7]

Cathedrals like Ely and York today provoke an emotional response from those who enter them, and indeed even a kind of commitment. They become a place where people connect with God. They do this of their own accord. When someone enters for the first time, it is as if the very stones speak: *'Behold!'* they say, *'lift up your eyes'*. These cathedrals and many other churches and chapels like them, are visible, tangible places which offer people space to fall in love with God; they were built to do this, and over 1,000 years later they still do. The Great West Window of York Minster presents what is known as 'The Heart of Yorkshire', a beautiful stained-glass window

7 A number of 'new monastic' communities have sprung up in in recent years providing space for those exploring the 'serious call' of God on their lives, and examining in community, how that call is lived out. See Chapter 8, above.

with a tracery in the shape of a heart. It is said locally that if a couple declare their love for each other under that window, their vow will hold forever.

What people see at Ely and in York sometimes provokes them to tears, and I have heard many stories from those, who after just a few visits, have come to love these places in a way which is almost beyond words: they become committed and come back year after year, day after day. A few years ago, an American couple, both previously stationed in Cambridgeshire in the military, brought their families back to Ely to give thanks for their marriage after ten years. They came with all the usual ups and downs that married life brings, but it was the cathedral that had prompted or provoked them to recall their vows, in its own inimitable way.

At Petertide, cathedrals are those places which help create new priests and deacons and help them make their vow of ordination, kneeling and prostrating themselves around the altar to make life-changing promises. These are serious promises which call those who make them to a 'devout and holy life', with the caveat that of course we are only human. Then, once a year, every deacon, priest and bishop in a diocese is invited back to renew their ordination vows during the Chrism Mass on Maundy Thursday. Myriads of white robes then gather around the altar as the clergy reaffirm the promises they have made, to recall what brought them to make those promises in the first place, and to pray for all that is yet to come in their wake.

The Vows as a Home for Beholden-ness

While formal public vows form the very foundation of any cathedral's activity, cathedrals can also create a space and context for others whose promises are as yet less formal but no less serious. Could these visible manifestations of the Church be considered places where vows might be conceived, where people first become beholden to God? Very often, as we say morning prayer in one of the side chapels as the formal expression of the Church in this place, and as an outworking of our own vows, people are quietly coming in and offering their own private prayers in another corner of the cathedral. Unbeknownst to us, there are plenty who speak to God in this place and practice their faith without the mediation of a priest or the foundation of a vow, it is as if heart calls to heart.

Indeed, we might reflect on how people will often remain quite intentionally at the fringes of regular, formal worship; they will not sit in the main body of the congregation, but rather just adjacent to it. They are almost deliberately on the edge, slightly out of view, simply sitting with their own thoughts and devotions. Nevertheless, the very witness of those who are vowed as practising Christians is, for them, an attractive sight to behold, and draws them and others in – albeit tentatively. It is perhaps like walking home on a cold winter's evening and passing by the windows of warmly homes lit from within with their enticing glow. They beckon and call and witness to something which offers security and contentment and hope. There is a yearning to be part of that community, a yearning to be on the inside which somehow seems beyond reach; it is a glimpse into something, and yet so many pull their scarf closer and walk onwards into the chill wind.

This tentative sensibility is particularly noticeable at services of Choral Evensong, and I do wonder whether the trope that the desire for 'anonymity' is a factor in cathedral growth, is now slightly out of date. It has often been suggested that people are attracted to large cathedrals because you can remain anonymous and invisible within them, but we might ask: invisible to whom? Their prayers are certainly not invisible to God. Having worked in two such cathedrals, I now think the reason people are drawn to these places is far more complex, and in part may be because people have the space in a cathedral to offer their own devotions, in their own way, in a place which is already built on vows: in this way, perhaps, others' vows can be accessed vicariously? They not only look through the window, but they are allowed in, just as they are. The wonder is that people are drawn into these sacred spaces in the first place – like moths to the light, they see the warm enticing glow inside, and they actually come in. But what next?

Maybe the hesitation is less about a desired anonymity and more about the fear of 'religion' and the fear of entering into the unknown rituals of the Church. Why not then just sit in the Quire and 'behold', soaking up the wonderful tradition of worship, the beautiful music, and the arresting, slightly archaic words without too much pressure to conform?

It is almost as if there is always another Church running alongside the official one, an invisible Church, a Church in the world where people make their own improvised communion with God in their own language, where people light candles and make their own promises and prayers without clerical intercession or interference. Perhaps this is why cathedrals are the surprise story of recent 'church growth' statistics? They are places where there is a simple space for you and God – face to face – gazing upon one another; and perhaps evensong, also a growing attraction, is a service in which people feel they are most able to experience God directly and personally, without being asked to undertake a visible sacramental act of Communion or explicit commitment. Could it be that cathedrals, and places like them, have a particular calling to act as a marker on the journey *towards* a vowed life? Perhaps they are places where people can fall in love with God, and even become – over time – mysteriously 'beholden'?

A First Call to a Devout and Holy Life

Living our lives in the way described by Law in the eighteenth century now seems extreme or even fanatical. We live in changing times, where commitment to religious organizations like the Church of England is seriously out of fashion. And yet, and yet ... there is plenty of evidence that people still yearn to know God, their hearts already open to the divine. It is almost as if people today are very happy to cut out the middle-man and go direct to the 'boss' (in the form of a 'spirituality' without 'religion', as the epithet goes). We certainly see this idea in action day by day in a cathedral context where it is always difficult to distinguish between tourists, visitors and pilgrims. People often enter a cathedral on their own terms: without expectation, and without expectation being put upon them. They make their own transaction with God, but that response may in due course become heart-bound: then they are suddenly caught up in a love which will not let them go. It's a divine 'meet-cute'.

I want to suggest, then, that *beholden-ness* is an appropriate way of describing the peculiar first calling (or first love) of what we might call the 'pre-Christian'; whereas a baptismal vow marks the moment when a Christian is actually born. *Beholden-ness* is the best word I can find presently to describe the way that many are drawn to the Christian *way of life*; and it's the best word I can find to describe the difficulty they may have in 'turning away' definitively and refusing to look on God, even in anger or despair, apathy or euphoria. It is the word that describes the first 'call' to duty, service, and sacrifice. We then continue to 'behold', and we continue to be 'beholden' to God.

Love Speaks to Love

Being a Christian is no longer an expectation of polite society; in fact being a Christian in contemporary Britain is more likely to provoke ridicule than respect. Today any commitment is very much an active choice, a decision which is made rather than a given; and that 'choice' which still many millions do make, warrants some unpacking. Today, it seems people do *choose* to be beholden to God while at the same time, God continues to enter into the lives of some without warning, like a thief in the night, stealing their hearts. The paradox in all of this talk about 'choice', of course, is that strictly speaking we do not initiate the choice at all; for we have been chosen by God before the world began, and commissioned to go out and bear fruit that will last. God sees us first: we are 'beheld' by God and then invited to respond. Nowhere is this clearer than in the historic faith journey of St Augustine, who acknowledges in his *Confessions* that God was with him all along, even though his own conscious and more explicit love came later.[8] God 'beheld'

8 'Late have I loved Thee, O Lord; and behold,
Thou wast within and I without, and there I sought Thee.
Thou was with me when I was not with Thee.

him first, and eventually he lifted up his eyes to see. If we need a classic exemplar of the long engagement, or someone who illustrates in their own life the pressure of 'beholden-ness' *prior* to a conscious commitment, we have it in Augustine. And that, of course, was the insight that fueled his profound understanding of the *prevenience* of grace.

The challenge for the Church of England today, in this strange post-modern, post-secular period of cultural half-belief, is this: how do we nurture this mysterious intimation of 'beholdenness' without destroying it in the process? When someone falls in love with God, even so strangely that it cannot be consciously identified as such, how can that love be sustained and nourished? Like the vine branches which need to be trained upon the frame, can the Church draw upon all of its traditions and resources to help people grow in their faith and bear fruit? How do we enable and encourage people to grow in friendship with God and in love for God's people?

How then do we encourage these spiritual seekers, these people touched by the love of God? How can we use and manifest the traditional vows of the Church to help the people who fall in love with God to live a consciously vowed life *to* God – in all that they do and think and say? What does a serious call, or a 'devotion', authentically look like, and how is that devotion to be shaped by the traditional vows which begin with a call to die with Christ in order that we be raised with him?

The modern, French Carmelite Thérèse of Lisieux (1873–97) memorably describes her own faith precisely as a falling in love with God. In her autobiographical writings, *The Story of a Soul*, [9] she narrates her life's journey from childhood to confession and outlines her understanding of how a commitment to Christ is made manifest in community, and in the everyday tasks of life: it has become a simple manual for those wishing to commit their whole life to Christ; it is an anchor and guide

Thou didst call, and cry, and burst my deafness.
Thou didst gleam, and glow, and dispell my blindness.'

St Augustine, 1943, *The Confessions of St Augustine*, translated by F. J. Sheed, New York: Sheed & Ward, p. 236 (X, 27).

9 St Thérèse of Lisieux, 2010, *Story of a Soul: The Autobiography of the Little Flower*, edited by Mother Agnes of Jesus, translated by Michael Day, Gastonia, NC: Tan Classics.

which isn't afraid to domesticate the spiritual. She writes of her complete and consuming devotion to God. It is a love like no other, and it is from this love, the love that well preceded her actual vows, that her life of service began. She was 'beholden' first, and 'avowed' second; and she understood that at the heart of the Church was love, from which all vocations emanated. As she put it in her own words:

> I saw that the Church must have a heart, that this heart must be on fire with love. I saw that it was love alone which moved her other members, and that were this love to fail, apostles would no longer spread the Gospel and martyrs would refuse to shed their blood. I saw that all vocations are summed up in love and that love is all in all, embracing every time and place because it is eternal.[10]

Likewise, it feels like we are starting again as we consider afresh in a post-modern, post-pandemic era the relation between coming to be 'beholden' (the initial, alluring, 'falling in love' with God), and the making of serious Christian vows. Christian vows continue to be made, of course, especially baptismal vows made on behalf of a child by those who are themselves often unsure about where they stand in a range of possibilities between half-belief, being incipiently drawn to be 'beholden', or making a full commitment. To claim that vows made in such a context are somehow magically and immediately efficacious would be wholly mistaken, as Augustine also saw with incisive vision. The objective *validity* of a sacramental vow (as in baptism) cannot be confused with its graced and efficacious *outworking*, whenever that may occur.[11] And there are formidable obstacles to this occurrence; there is such a lapse in understanding of the Christian narrative, such a loss of shared meaning, that most do not even know who 'Jesus' is. But if Christ calls, as he still does and will, how do people know that the Church may still be the right place where they can respond? How can they know that the Church is where people can fully explore the love of

10 St Thérèse, *Story of a Soul*, p. 163.

11 Any vow taken requires a daily re-commitment, whether that is baptism, confirmation, marriage or ordination.

God that has been kindled within them and where permanent vows can be nurtured, encouraged and cherished?

The Church of England may be in catastrophic numerical decline, but thankfully, God isn't. Still the question presses: could the offering of the formal vows of the Church become a home for being beholden to God at every stage of our life's journey, an anchor to which we can cling in the storm – and can public vows become the means of *ratifying* that 'serious call to live a devout and holy life' as an acknowledged Christian?

What has not changed today is the seriousness with which a life beholden to God is lived out and made manifest by a public vow. In earlier generations the making of the vow might have been a merely cultural convention, but today, this is not purely a consumer choice: it is a wholehearted, counter-cultural commitment, and a 'serious call'. God is for life, and not just for Christmas, and people seem to sense that today with even greater force. The important thing, therefore, is for those who call themselves Christian to ratify and articulate the way in which they have become mysteriously 'beholden' to God, and then live out their public vow in their daily lives so that a way of life becomes the vow, and the vow becomes a way of life. For all the church's failings and ambiguities in these strange times, vows are once again becoming matters for serious concern and even mysterious attraction, imbued with the initiating divine allure that alone can tell the story of grace, repentance, and salvation.

Two Poems

RACHEL MANN

Edmund Newey writes: A recent symposium on poetry, faith and spiritality bore the title Making Nothing Happen.[1] *The title alludes to W. H. Auden's famous line in the poem, 'In Memory of W.B. Yeats': 'For poetry makes nothing happen'.*[2] *The aphorism is particularly apt for verse that operates in the territory of religion. In the same way that God is 'no thing', but rather the ungrounded ground of the Being of all that is, so the poetry that arises out of the life of faith and worship will guide us away from the consuming instrumental logic of our daily lives into the embrace of the divine. The small selection of two of Rachel Mann's poems here presented*[3] *does just this, and makes a fitting conclusion to a book on the 'vowed life'. Like vows themselves, these poems take the simple stuff of our daily round and open it up to the transcendent realm of God's grace.*

1 D'Costa, Gavin, Nesbitt, Eleanor, Pryce, Mark, Shelton, Ruth and Slee, Nicola, 2014, *Making Nothing Happen: Five Poets Explore Faith and Spirituality*, London: Routledge.

2 Auden, W. H., 1976, *Collected Poems*, edited by Edward Mendelson, London: Faber & Faber, p. 248.

3 These poems are taken from Rachel Mann's 2019 collection, *A Kingdom of Love*, Manchester: Carcanet Press, and reprinted here by kind permission of the publisher.

The Ordinal

I've lived for the feelings of others,
That's a listening of sorts,

What have I learnt? That self
Is bitumen, black as tar,

Oh, how slowly we flow, oh
How slowly we flow, we crack with age.

I've lived for the feelings of others,
A philosophy of sorts. I've heard

Self give up its final word,
Coughs and whispers in

Hospitals and nursing homes.
Oh, how slowly we flow, oh.

Collect for Purity

I try to form prayer's capital word
On my tongue. O sweet imagination
Give it shape enough! *Love!*

Love should taste of something,
The sea, I think, brined and unsteady,
Of scale and deep and all we crawled out from.

Of first day, the Spirit's début,
The frantic dove torn apart,
Her feathers ash on Eden.

Yet of that of which we cannot speak
We must pass over in silence –
Selah!

The Spirit itself maketh intercession for us
With groanings
Which cannot be uttered.

Afterword: The Vowed Life

JUSTIN WELBY
THE ARCHBISHOP OF CANTERBURY

I am grateful that the members of the Littlemore Group have taken time to share such rich reflections on the subject of the 'vowed life', not least because these contributions challenge us to see in the specific charisms of the Religious lessons for all of us who are Christians. The radical, costly and counter-cultural venture that is the life of the Religious models to us the radical, costly and counter-cultural decision of every single Christian at baptism.

In a world where those of us with privilege are assailed with choices, the only compelling choice we have to offer is being bound to the glorious freedom of Jesus Christ. I am convinced that any healthy desire for the Church to grow and be a more effective leaven in wider society will not be realized through a watering down of the demands of Christian discipleship or by somehow making the Church into an enticing lifestyle option. This is why I have been committed to the launch and development of the Community of St Anselm, a new Religious community bringing young people together in prayer and service at Lambeth Palace. The young people that I encounter are seeking a spirituality with rigour, vitality, and truthfulness, through stages of life, and death, and in serious community. The Community of St Anselm draws from around the Anglican Communion and therefore brings us face to face with some of those stories without privilege: of poverty, war, and even persecution. *Their* presence, and *their* prayers, uphold us as staff at

Lambeth Palace, being the fundamental liturgy, work of God, of all our work.

Paradoxically, as the Authorized Version has it, 'the love of Christ *constraineth* us' (2 Cor. 5.14): the reconciliation of all things goes by way of the cross, so that losing our own lives becomes the gateway to incalculable new life. In David Ford's magisterial new commentary on John's Gospel,[1] he reminds us of the central question that Jesus poses: 'What do you want?', or 'What do you desire?' Religious communities put that question front and centre for the church, and to the world. The lessons of Religious life in history, of the vows that we make in different ways across the life of the Church, and the explorations of new Religious communities, are all brought together in this remarkable volume that we may indeed see Jesus Christ anew, and find our desires shaped towards the source of all that is good, true and beautiful.

1 Ford, David F., 2021, *The Gospel of John: A Theological Commentary*, Ada, MI: Baker Academic.

A Note on the Littlemore Group and Its Conferences

The Littlemore Group was originally founded in 2005 by Sarah Coakley and Samuel Wells, and brought together a number of parish-based Anglican priest-theologians with one Anglican Religious, Sr Judith, SLG, to think afresh about the enduring significance of parish life for Anglican theology and spirituality. In an era when academic theology and parish life seemed to be drifting apart, our project was to re-root theology into the life and prayer of the parish, and indeed to re-enrich it thereby via our own theological fellowship and writing, and by our reflection both on the riches of Anglican tradition and on the particular parochial challenges of our 'post-modern' era. (We aimed for a 'light touch' in our reliance on the liveliness of parish vignettes, but also at a depth and rigour of theological analysis that shunned academic obfuscation.) Right from the start, too, we saw the issue of the concomitant renewal of Anglican Religious life as endemic to our endeavour.

When we first began working together we were greatly heartened by the support of the then Archbishop of Canterbury, Rowan Williams, and later by his successor, Justin Welby; and most importantly we were sustained by the established discipline of our own residential and day-meetings, roughly twice a year. These have always involved, as crucial elements: silent and liturgical prayer (office), eucharistic worship, liturgical and chamber music, poetry-reading, simple but excellent meals, mutual support, and a *lot* of laughter. It has not been uncommon for members to admit that, in the face of really difficult parish and community circumstances, this Group and its shared prayer and humour have been vital for their courage and survival. Over the years the membership has shifted and changed a little year by year, with a deliberate intention to include new and younger voices on a regular basis, including those representing the full range of Anglican 'churchmanships'. But almost always the group has remained about 12 in number (that having a good dominical precedent, we felt!), and with roughly equal numbers of men and women. For most of our book projects we have specially invited one or more 'outsiders' to the Group who have been especially qualified to help us; in the case of this book, Dr Petà Dunstan, an expert on the history and contemporary witness of Anglican Religious life, has been a mainstay and an enormous source of wisdom for our reflections.

Over the years between 2005 and 2019 (when Sarah Coakley re-emigrated back to the United States) the Littlemore Group has in all produced five volumes together, of which this is the fifth and last in this series.[1] It is also the book on which the Group has expended most time and energy, spanning a considerable number of years of reflection and discussion. The project was initiated at a memorable residential meeting at the Sisters of Bethany's house in Portsmouth in 2013, during which sojourn we also spent time in Alex Hughes's then parishes (St Peter's and St Luke's, Southsea). We remember eating delicious fish and chips out of newspaper in his church-hall, and simultaneously watching a showing of the remarkable French film about the Thiberine Cisterican martyrs, *Of Gods and Men*. The book project continued to take shape, in the form of draft chapters, when we met next residentially in 2016 at Alnmouth, Northumberland, this time in the care of the Anglican Franciscans there: what a cold time of year 'we had of it' there in January; but along with our office, silence and Eucharist with the brothers, and our animated discussions around the wood

1 The earlier books were: Wells, Samuel, and Sarah Coakley (eds), 2008, *Praying for England: Priestly Presence in Contemporary Culture*, London: Continuum; Ward, Frances, and Sarah Coakley (eds), 2012, *Fear and Friendship: Anglicans Engaging with Islam*, London: Continuum; Martin, Jessica, and Sarah Coakley (eds), 2016, *For God's Sake: Re-Imagining Priesthood and Prayer in a Changing Church*, Norwich: Canterbury Press; and Ward, Frances, and Richard Sudworth (eds), 2019, *Holy Attention: Preaching in Today's Church*, Norwich: Canterbury Press.

fire, we enjoyed bracing walks to Dunstanburgh Castle and a visit to the shrine of Aidan in Bamburgh. While another Littlemore book project on preaching was also brewing, we met again in 2018 at St Stephen's House, Oxford (earlier the motherhouse of the Society of St John the Evangelist), and, sharing our daily prayer in the sparse original chapel at the top of the building, we continued to discuss and hone the chapters that now make up this book. Finally, after a lengthy and exacting editorial process, the cumulative arguments of the volume fell into place.

There are a number of people we must thank personally for supporting us in writing and publishing this book. First, both Archbishops of Canterbury in the period involved, Rowan Williams and Justin Welby, gave generously of their insights but also supported us financially for our residential conferences. So too did the St Andrew's Trust and Hymns Ancient & Modern which both gave generous grants. And most of us were individually supported by episcopal and diocesan funding sources, which helped our members with travel money and small bursaries for our residential meetings. But overall we managed 'on a shoe-string'; and this kept reminding us how rich can be the outcomes from very modest financial resources.

We have learned an enormous amount from all the Anglican Religious who have given us hospitality and fed their wisdom into our reflections, especially Br. Sam, SSF, and his Franciscan brethren; the Sisters of Bethany, Southsea; the Sisters of the Love of God, Fairacres, Oxford; the Community of St John the Divine (then at Alum Rock, Birmingham, now in Marston); and the Community of St Anselm, Lambeth Palace. Sarah Coakley would also like to express her personal indebtedness to the Community of the Resurrection, Mirfield, and to the Society of St John the Evangelist, Cambridge, MA, USA.

We acknowledge with thanks permission to use quotations from T. S. Eliot, 1942, 'Little Gidding', in *Four Quartets*, London: Faber and Faber, used in Chapter 9 of this book.

We would like finally to mention our deep gratitude to the editorial staff of Canterbury Press, and especially to Christine Smith, for her enthusiasm, patience and notable efficiency.

Index of Names and Subjects

Printed in the USA
CPSIA information can be obtained
at www.ICGtesting.com
JSHW021126161223
53804JS00006B/41